THE MIGHTY MUSTARD BUSH

THE MIGHTY MUSTARD BUSH

Kenneth Guentert

RESOURCE PUBLICATIONS, INC.
San Jose, California

Editorial director: Kenneth Guentert
Managing editor: Kathi Drolet
Copy editor: Elizabeth J. Asborno
Art director: Terri Ysseldyke-All

Photo credit: author photo—Perry Chow

Library of Congress Cataloging in Publication Data
Guentert, Kenneth.
  The mighty mustard bush / Kenneth Guentert.
    p.   cm.
  "These chapters originally appeared in "Final blessing,"
Kenneth Guentert's column in Modern liturgy
magazine"—
    ISBN 0-89390-184-9 : $8.95
    1. Sermons—Outlines, syllabi, etc. 2. Catholic
Church—Sermons. 3. Sermons, American.   I. Title.
BX1756.A1G78 1991
264'.02—dc20   90-47185

5 4 3 2 1 | 94 93 92 91

To the Gonzo Exegete,
who opened the Book for me,
May you live long and prosper.

Contents

PART III: FEASTS AND SEASONS

PART IV: PRAYER AND RITUAL

PART V: RECONCILIATION

Preface

As I read over the pages proof for this book, I realized how much it reflects my personal journey in the '80s.

As the decade started, I was beginning something of a new life. I had just left the *National Catholic Reporter* to try my hand at freelancing and writing my own newsletter, *Body&Soul*. The newsletter never amounted to much, but I learned to write and to make spirituality concrete (*Body&Soul's* first issue was on compost spirituality).

During that period of my life, I met someone who was to have a tremendous impact on my thinking. The Gonzo Exegete, to whom I dedicate this book, was working a government job at the time, even though he was an ordained minister in the Reformed Church of America and just completing doctoral studies in scripture at the University of Iowa. We met at a party and quickly discovered a mutual interest in drinking and Deuteronomy. Actually, my interest was somewhat broadly in religion, but that was enough for Gonzo to turn me on to Deuteronomy. In no time at all, I was an addict. Gonzo introduced me to what he called "Hebrew thinking," which he contrasted to the abstract "Greek thinking" of someone like Paul. Hebrew, the language, lends itself to punning (words come from three-letter roots and look like several other words) and concrete images. The Hebrews, originally, could not even think abstractly. They were always trying to explain abstract concepts by saying things like, "the kingdom of heaven is like a woman who lost her marbles." This is definitely good news for a writer.

Gonzo also showed me that I could approach something like Genesis with a fresh eye, unencumbered, more or less, with the Christian baggage I had been taught. I could look at the Adam and Eve passage, for example, much as a Jew might. Suddenly, whole new meanings opened up. Also good for a writer. And he taught me that the Gospel could be seen as commentary on Hebrew scriptures rather than the other way around. Voila! The Gospel began to come alive in ways it never had before. Suddenly, Jesus began to take on some interesting outlines. He wore a tallit, maybe had side curls, and zipped in and out of Jerusalem for Jewish holidays. Amazing!

Not long after Gonzo and I met, I got a lucky break. *Notre Dame* magazine asked me to go to Israel to cover an archeological dig at Capernaum, co-sponsored by the university. Gonzo, insanely jealous at my good fortune, signed up to go along. So there we were, mixing it up with Jews and Arabs at the site where Jesus called Peter and Andrew to sit at his feet. This gave my overactive writer's imagination some ground on which to stand. Holy ground. And the Bible made still more sense.

Back home in Illinois, I had agreed to teach religion to some sixth graders. This was the class nobody wanted. I got no instructions, because nobody had any to give. I did the best I could over the next three years and had a ball. The sixth-grade text focused on the Bible. We never got past Exodus, but the kids managed to teach me what it must have been like in the wilderness. They grounded me, too, and I still feel that the kids have taught me more than anyone else about scripture. With the possible exception of Gonzo. But then Gonzo was a kid, too. These adventures helped my writing and that led me, eventually, to San Jose and *Modern Liturgy*. As editor, I have a column and struggle to make what I know about scripture and living pertinent to people whose job it is to make liturgy better. These columns eventually led to this book.

Shortly after moving to San Jose, the RCIA coordinator in my home parish invited me to join the team. Three years later, I would move on to help the pastor begin a program for returning Catholics. These experiences moved me into the heart of a process that is changing the church and, among other things, taught me that everyone's story is important. Even mine. — KG.

Part I:
In the Beginning

The Big Fat God

Occasion: *General*
א

You can use words every day for years without really knowing what they mean.

Take the word "glory." I hadn't thought about it until the publisher, who also ought to know better, admitted he's always been puzzled by the line, "We praise you for your glory."

We praise people for their good grades, their fast cars, their fancy clothes, their sexual prowess, their accomplishments, and their ability to listen to our troubles—but what does it mean to praise someone, God in particular, for his or her glory?

The word is a translation from the Hebrew, *kavod* (sounds like abode), which originally meant "weight." Middle Eastern potentates, it seems, were men of great girth and many goods. The bigger the sheik, the more the camels, the more the kavod. From this, kavod came to mean "power." We still use the expression, "to throw one's weight around," to indicate the use of power. The '60s use of the adjective, "heavy," caught the spirit of kavod rather nicely.

Thus, to praise God's glory is to marvel at the great weight and awesome power of a magnificent hunk of divinity. Heavy, man! Out of sight!

Praising someone's kavod is usually exuberant rather than ponderous, spontaneous rather than formal, even if the praisemaking occurs in ritual form. Think of the Bedouin host throwing himself on the ground, as Abraham did with the three strangers, and heaping words of praise on his visitors. Or, in our culture, think of the crowds that greeted Ronald Reagan at the end of his first term. "Four more years! Four more years!" is nothing less than an American way of acknowledging the kavod of an incumbent president.

However, for the Hebrew people it was important to give "glory in the highest" only to the supreme potentate: YHWH. No earthly king, no president, no political party, no platform, no ideology, no nuclear freeze has the ultimate power to save or to liberate. Thinking otherwise is to stumble toward idolatry.

Still, it is important to give kavod to human beings. God does, crowning human creatures with "glory and honor" (Ps 8) and commanding them in turn to "honor" (Hebrew: *kavod*) their parents. Ultimately, though, the command is to set aside a special place for the stranger, the poor, the oppressed. It is God's trick, born of the wisdom that kavod does not "trickle down" but flows up. Thus, we start by honoring the lowest of the low, whom the stories all say may be the Lord disguised.

Eden: The First Idle Threat

Occasion: *1st Sunday of Lent (A)*

א

Everybody knows about the apple in the Garden of Eden story.

But if you look closely, it isn't there, any more than the more culturally apt pomegranate is there, except in the imagination.

Nor are there animals in the Christmas story, at least as told by Matthew and Luke, but what would a Christmas play be without the shyest kids costumed in sheets covered with cotton balls, bleating and crawling around the auditorium on all fours? Tradition and the human imagination filled a stable (also not mentioned) with an ox and an ass and lambs.

The human imagination—or perhaps the lack of it—also tells us that Adam and Eve lost their immortality in the Garden of Eden.

But that isn't the story either.

To be sure, God tells Adam and Eve that they will die as soon as they eat from the tree of knowledge. (Gn 2:16)

They ate and they died all right, but some 930 years later, which is not exactly dropping dead on the spot. And if the fall-from-immortality theory is right, one wonders about the logic that allowed the perpetrators of that dastardly crime to live longer than we who merely inherited their spiritual genes. 'Taint fair.

With apologies to St. Augustine, I find the story easier to understand when I see the God of this story as parent (or parents—the text is plural in key places) and Adam and Eve as children. What we have then is the world's first-recorded idle threat. Do this and you will drop dead, the bogeyman will get you, you'll get "what for." Children grow up when they quit believing parental baloney—which is what happens when they eat from the tree of knowledge.

Adam and Eve would have died even if they hadn't eaten from the tree of knowledge. To live forever, they would have had to eat from the tree of life, and they were too busy getting an education to live forever.

Maybe they would have gotten around to it. The possibility certainly occurred to God, who kicked Adam out lest he "put out his hand to take fruit from the tree of life also, and thus eat of it and live forever." (Gn 3:22) What are we to make of an insecure, jealous God, who seems afraid at this point to share life with the human? It is not a pretty picture.

Again, the story is understandable to me when I see God as a parent booting the overgrown kids out of the house lest they hang around forever. What looks like punishment is a parent being a parent, pushing the kids out of the nest, making them fly on their own.

Which reminds me of another assumption I used to make about the story; namely, that Eve ran out and snarfed the forbidden fruit the minute God told her not to.

I learned from some eleven-year-olds I was privileged to teach that this may not have been the case.

To teach them the Garden of Eden story, I installed a mysterious black pot in the middle of the room and attached a note telling whomever not to look inside unless they were prepared to drop dead.

Of course, they looked, but it took them three classes to work up the nerve. In the meantime, I nearly went crazy trying to figure out schemes to make them look. I wound up appointing someone to tempt them.

The episode taught me 1) that Adam and Eve could have been in the garden for years before they took that first bite and 2) God probably wanted Eve to eat the fruit.

I'm not sure why yet, except that if she hadn't, the Bible would have been a very short book.

Abraham: The Father of Hospitality

Occasion: *16th Sunday of the Year (C)*
א

As a child, the only thing I knew about Abraham was that he made his kid carry a bunch of wood up a mountain and then tried to stab him to death.

This meant Abraham had great faith, the teacher said.

I hoped my father did not have such great faith.

The teacher, of course, explained that God was trying to test Abraham and that Abraham had passed. God never would have let Abraham kill his own child.

Maybe just scare the hell out of him.

I can think of three reasons why we tell this story to children.

One is that like "Rock a Bye Baby," the tale allows adults to express their hostility to children in a socially acceptable way. I confess that I myself passed on the story of Abraham and Isaac to some eleven-year-olds with rather more glee than it deserved.

Another is that it works. This is a visceral story told to visceral people (children) who respond, if you give them half a chance, with fear, anger, and hostility—depending on whether they identify with Abraham, Isaac, Sarah, or God.

A third is that the story fits our pre-Vatican II liturgical emphasis on the Eucharist as sacrifice.

I don't want to neglect the sacrificial aspects of the Eucharist, but given the times and the renewed emphasis on the Eucharist as a meal, we should begin to teach children and adults about the Abraham of hospitality.

The key story is the visit of the three strangers to Abraham by the oaks of Mamre. (Gn 18) Notice that Abraham runs out to meet the strangers and, as is typical today of Middle Eastern hospitality, presents himself as servant. "Sir, if I may ask you this Favor, do not go on past your servant." (Gn 18:3)

Abraham sees that his guests find the shade of a tree, water for washing their feet, bread, milk, and meat. Though others prepare the fare, Abraham serves the guests himself.

Though the menu changes (substitute wine for milk, fish for the fatted calf) the key elements of hospitality are repeated throughout the Bible, from Lot's entertainment of the two strangers one chapter later to the Last Supper and beyond.

The host is always generous, always welcoming, always servant. Jesus extends Abrahamic hospitality to its logical conclusion when he washes the guests' feet himself.

Among Jews and Moslems, Abraham is remembered as a man of hospitality as much as a man of faith. In the Talmud, it is remembered that Abraham planted an orchard, which "was not an orchard as we understand the word but an inn" and that he "made known the name of God among the heathens" by his hospitality.

When his guests tried to thank him, he said, "Do not thank me, for I am not the owner of this place; thank God who made the heavens and the earth."

Abrahamic hospitality is expansive, meant for strangers and especially the poor. "Remember how kindly Abraham treated the three angels whom he thought were men," says the Talmud. "When (the poor) enter thy house, receive them with a friendly glance and set immediately before them bread and salt."

As we try to convince our brothers and sisters that we, as assembly, are the host of the eucharistic celebration, we might point out that Abraham, not God, is the host of the heavenly banquet.

We may not be asked to walk up the mountain with Abraham, but we are asked to sit in his seat.

Good Ol' Elijah

Occasion: *32d Sunday of the Year (B)*
א

I'm sure there have been sermons in Christian churches about Elijah, but I've never heard one. I heard a preacher say the name once, but it turned out to be a reference to a football player.

Too bad. Jesus, the Gospel says, was mistaken for Elijah, which suggests we'd find out more about Jesus if we studied the muscular wonder-worker whose name means "YHWH is God."

There's an opportunity in the first reading for this Sunday. (1 Kgs 17) It tells how Elijah multiplied meal and oil for the widow of Zarephath.

Here are some things I noticed about the passage.

1. It is eucharistic, reminding us of the multiplication of loaves and fishes story. Actually, we have it backwards: the loaves and fishes story reminded Jesus' Jewish followers of the widow of Zarephath story and of similar tales. Belief in the miraculous increase in certain products, especially oil and wheat, were and are prevalent in the Middle East. Each village seems to have its own story, going back to some person long dead who actually saw the deed. No one knows how the miracles happen; only that they do and that the miracles prove that "all good things come from God." Even though no comparable stories exist in the West—with the

11

possible exception of stories about monster zucchini crops — Eucharist needs to be a celebration of the generosity of God.

2. The great deed is a physical one. Utterly concrete. The spiritual point—the generosity of God—is not separate from the physical act of feeding a hungry widow. Eucharist cannot become disconnected from the physical world and retain its power.

3. The beneficiary of the great deed is the host. She not only receives, but gives, and quite possibly receives *only* because she gives. In the lectionary, the story is tied to the Gospel story of the widow's mite. Same point. Eucharist demands hospitality.

4. The beneficiary of the great deed is an individual. Earlier prophets performed wonders but almost always on behalf of the people as a whole. Elijah was a political prophet, railing against the Northern Kingdom's worship of Baal, but his miracle on behalf of the widow is an interlude and serves no political purpose. Elijah did not solve world hunger; he fed a widow. So does the Eucharist.

5. The woman is a gentile, a Phoenician from what is now Lebanon. Luke's Jesus was almost killed for telling Nazareth that Elijah was sent only to this foreigner even though "there were many widows in Israel" during the great drought. (4:25) The story is a reminder that Eucharist reaches beyond one's own community and, less happily, that it is not always the source of unity we intend it to be. Hospitality is eternally unfinished.

Part II:
Jesus and Family

Holy Family:
It Ain't What It Used to Be

Occasion: *Feast of the Holy Family*
א

One of my ambitions in life is to write the Great American Jesus Novel.

I'll probably never get around to finishing it, other deadlines being what they are, but I've done some character development on the Holy Family that seems appropriate.

The Family: My Holy Family is an extended family composed of many relatives. Elizabeth, Mary's kinswoman, and her husband Zechariah play important roles in the beginning of Luke's Gospel as does their son John in the life of Jesus. Luke's infancy narrative implies the existence of Joseph's relatives in Bethlehem, and Matthew 13:55 speaks explicitly of Jesus' sisters and brothers (the latter by name: James and Joseph and Simon and Judas.) James, referred to in Galatians 1:19 as "the brother of the Lord," became the leader of the Christian community in Jerusalem.

I haven't decided whether to make these brothers and sisters by blood or to preserve Mary's eternal virginity by making the brothers and sisters "cousins" or "half-brothers" or "adopted." I just know I can't dance away from the strong kinship implied in the words "brother and sister." In short, my Holy Family is much larger than three.

Holy: My Holy Family is not holy in the sense of "nice" but in the sense of "set apart," the meaning of the Hebrew *kodesh*. None of the holy individuals in Hebrew scriptures, let alone the holy people of Israel, were nice. Or perfect. Or particularly loving. They were holy in the sense of marked out for a special relationship with God. They did what they had to do in order to keep the covenant with God, even if it meant a little conniving, lusting, or killing. Holiness was not acquired by good behavior but given by God to people who were—and are—no different from us. Holiness is not so much normative (we should behave like these holy people) as descriptive (these holy people are like us). They are ancestors, containing our flaws, our virtues, and the seeds of our faith.

So my Holy Family is like all families. There is dissension, jealousy, bickering. *The Jerome Biblical Commentary* for Mark 3:20-35 suggests a deeply divided family, with some relatives siding with scribes who thought Jesus was possessed and/or out of his mind while Jesus asks, more in sorrow than in anger, "Who are my mother and [my] brothers?" (Mk 3:33) Answering his own question, Jesus identifies not his blood relatives but his students as his new family. This suggests that Jesus headed a school, not uncommon throughout Jewish history, and that his work created some tension between himself and his relatives.

Mary: My image of Mary is influenced by apparition lore. She always seems to appear to peasant people, often to children, but always on the side of the poor against the powers that be. As a result, my Mary is a crusty peasant woman, perhaps with a hatred of Rome and a sympathy for Galilean zealots. "He has thrown down the rulers from their thrones," she exclaims in Luke 1:52, "and lifted up the lowly." My Jesus gets his sympathy for the oppressed from her.

Joseph: The Talmud refers to a man who goes up to read Torah in the synagogue as a "carpenter" or "carpenter's son." My Joseph, therefore, is not a carpenter (Mary is more "blue collar" than Joseph) but a synagogue leader, a learned man, who makes sure his son knows Torah by heart by the time he came of age ("Did you not know that I must be in my Father's house?" — Lk 2:49). Jesus gets his education and his affinity for legal debate from his old man.

Jesus: My Jesus, as you might have guessed by now, is very Jewish. But this might be a surprise. I do not think of him as a young man. Tradition has him starting his ministry at the age of 30. For us, 30 is young. For the first-century Jew, 30 was a time when a man could retire from his profession and study Torah full-time. You don't have to agree with this, but isn't it interesting to imagine Jesus as a tallit-wearing graybeard instead of the blue-eyed youth of Hollywood portrayals?

The Mother:
Woman with No Name

Doug Adams, a professor of art and religion at the Pacific School of Religion, likes to show students a renaissance painting of the Blessed Mother and the child Jesus looking away from each other. The painting, he said, hints at the tension and even estrangement that is perfectly consistent with this relationship as it is depicted in the non-infancy-narrative portion of the Gospels.

Consider these four stories in which, by the way, Mary is rather pointedly mentioned not by name but by role.

1. I want to live with my father.

In Luke 2, Jesus disappears and is found, after three days, sitting with the teachers discoursing about Torah. When his mother, like any mother, asks why he has treated his custodial parents so rudely, Jesus pulls a line out of the stepchildren's manual, "You shoulda known I'd be in my father's house." Yes, maybe, but she didn't understand, even when he went more or less obediently back home, and she pondered stuff. And wondered if the kid was growing up too fast—or too slowly.

2. Mother who?

The synoptic Gospels all contain the story of the
crowd telling Jesus that his mother and brothers
were waiting to see him only to hear him retort,
"Who are my mother and [my] brothers?" In the
stories (Mt 12, Mk 3, Lk 8), he never does go to meet
them. This is a rude man. In spirit, this harsh story
must be linked to other passages that place kingdom
ties before kinship ties. (Mt 10:37, for example)

3. Lady, you're nobody to me.

The story of the wedding feast at Cana (Jn 2)
contains the mother's simple statement of fact,
"They have no wine," followed by Jesus' plainly
distancing remark. "Woman, how does your concern
affect me? My hour has not yet come." (Jn 2:4) The
title, "Woman," has the formal impact of "Madam"
or "Lady" and would not ordinarily have been used
by a son to his mother. That the remark is meant to
distance is obvious from the line that follows. Of
course, Jesus does finally go along with the program
but, as Doug Adams asks, "What kind of son, when
asked to help with the dishes, says, 'Madam, you're
nothing to me. This is no time for dishes.' "

4. I'm nobody to you.

Finally, there is the curious story of Jesus' dying
words to his mother and the beloved disciple. (Jn 19)
Again, he addresses her in that formal non-filial way.
"Woman, behold, your son." (Jn 19:26) And to the
disciple he says, "Behold, your mother." (Jn 19:27)
Was he taking care of his mom (she had sons or kin
to look after her already)? Was he taking care of the
beloved disciple (he had his own kin)? Or was he
distancing himself again from his mother. Madam,
look away from me; look at him. The passage reflects

more intimacy between the community of the
beloved disciple and Jesus' mother than it does
between Jesus and his mother.

Perhaps that is the point. In the life of Jesus, it was
the father who was important. In the life of Christ,
embodied in the community, the mother came into
her own. In Acts 1:1-14, after the ascension, she even
gets her name back.

Joseph:
A Jew, Not a Geek

Occasion: *Feast of St. Joseph*

א

I've thought for a long time that Joseph's image could use some work.

You figure. What's your image of him? Really.

Here's a blue-collar guy who finds out his girl is pregnant, marries her even though he is not the father, stays with her even though he can never have sex with her for as long as he lives, raises her son, and then dies.

Now is this a nice guy or what?

Is this a geek or what?

I mean, this man has no spunk. He's a bigger sacrificial animal than his kid. Everybody can agree that Joseph is a saint, and that he's a great model for the wimp of the '80s, who supports super-woman who manages to hold down jobs as both mother of millennia *and* queen of heaven, but do we really admire this bozo? I don't.

The good news is that this image of Joseph is not biblical, at least if I'm reading Ray Brown correctly. In the November issue of *Worship* magazine, Brown does an exegetical study of Matthew 1:18-25 that portrays Joseph as essentially a man who sought to preserve every "jot and tittle" of the Law in his behavior.

It was this desire—or at least the desire to portray him so—that explains Joseph's intent to divorce Mary quietly. (Joseph and Mary, apparently, were in that transitional period between formal marriage and living together.) With this intent, Joseph indicated a complex understanding of the Law. On one hand, his decision showed a sensitivity to Israel's understanding of the sanctity of marriage in that Mary's loss of virginity might have been considered adultery. (Dt 22:20-21) On the other hand, his decision indicated his sensitivity to the "protective character" of the Law, which acknowledged that virginity could be lost voluntarily (Dt 22:20-24) or by force. (Dt 22:25-27) So Joseph planned to do the righteous thing, but not at Mary's expense. He would demand no trial.

Matthew is presenting this Joseph as a model for Christians who would reconcile "a profound obedience to the Law with an acceptance of Jesus," says Brown. "In the church of our own times where a mention of law may evoke legalism (either because of past memories or because of unimaginative enforcement by those who should be interpreting), Matthew's sensitive description of a Law-obedient or righteous Joseph gives new importance to the invocation 'St. Joseph.' "

That's a Joseph I can get behind.

This change in image links up with a radically different image of Jesus that emerges from *Rediscovering Passover* by Joseph Stallings (Resource Publications, Inc., 1988). Stallings' Jesus is not a youth. In those days, retirement age was thirty, after which men took up the study of Torah full time. Jesus was, therefore, an elder. He was not only a rabbi and the leader of a synagogue, but the head of a school, or a collection of synagogues.

Some of the evidence for that is in Acts 1:15, which counts 120 men in the upper room at the time of Pentecost. As Stallings sees it, the number comes from the twelve apostles, who each led a synagogue composed of the requisite *minyan* of ten men. So those 120 men, along with their women and children, would have gathered in the upper room earlier for the Last Supper. And they would have eagerly followed the instructions of their rabbi who led the seder just as his father had done before him.

Jesus, the Jew

Occasion: *General*
א

Among the new images of Jesus that are gaining strength among Christians is that of Jesus, the Jew.

"New image" may be a bit of misnomer for a man who was born, reared, and executed as Jew.

Yet the image seems to come to an embarrassing number of Christians as a great surprise—as if it were somehow odd that Jesus recited the Shema and wore the tallit instead of said the rosary and wore a cassock.

But the reaction to Jesus' Jewishness is as much a part of the Christian story as the fact itself.

The way I teach the story—his and ours—is that Jesus became a way to the God of Abraham, Isaac, and Jacob for the nations of the world. So that whereas Jews get to the covenant by birth, the nations get to the covenant through Jesus (or to be very ecumenical, through the Qu'ran, but that is another story).

Arguably, Peter's submission to Paul's contention that Christians no longer needed to practice Jewish tradition may have been necessary to open the messiah—already Greekified as the Christ—to the nations. But in practice, that decision helped create a Christian community that quickly became non-Jewish at best, anti-Jewish at worst, and so pig-ignorant of Jewish tradition they could use a Hebrew word like Hosanna in their sacred liturgy without knowing what it meant ("save us").

Now, inspired to some extent by the lovely document, *Nostra Aetate*, the church has begun the task of making amends to Jews.

But there is more to making amends than acknowledging that Jews did not kill Christ (very liberal of us) or that we grew out of Judaism (and thank God have grown past it). We have to make amends to ourselves by examining the extent to which we are called to be Jewish. In other words, we have to get back to the dispute that originally divided Peter and Paul.

If Jesus were really Jewish—fundamentally Jewish; if he were circumcised and dedicated to the God of Abraham, Isaac, and Jacob; if he knew and studied Torah, the Writings, and the Prophets; if he spoke in the synagogue; if he wore the tallit and said the Shema; if he traveled to Jerusalem on the great feasts; if he tried to make the Law come alive by wrestling with it, challenging it, and telling stories about; if his heart burned to make the lame walk, the deaf hear, and the blind see; if people thought of him as Moses, or Elijah, or a King David, or a prophet; if he died at Roman hands like thousands of other Jews; if Jesus were Jewish at his core, are we not called to the same core?

The wellspring of Judaism is Torah, the Law, the first five books of the Bible. If Jesus were Jewish, and it seems that he was, the same would have been true for him. Yet we have often acted, thanks to St. Paul, as if the Spirit of Jesus and the Spirit of Torah were fundamentally different. They are not. They are the same.

This is not to say we need to mimic contemporary Jews. They have a Talmudic tradition that we do not have and we have a Gospel tradition that they do not have. Our interpretations of Torah may differ. We may not want to put little scrolls on our foreheads and wrists or avoid mixing dairy and meat products together, for example, but we surely need to pay more attention to Torah than does either of our lectionaries.

Like Father, Like Son

Occasion: *3rd Sunday of Lent (B)*

א

What do the Ten Commandments and the story of Jesus driving the moneychangers from the temple have in common?

Nothing originally, but they have been linked in the lectionary for the Third Sunday of Lent. And there's nothing like wrestling with a couple of unrelated texts for inspiring creativity.

Exodus 20:1-17 is about as straightforward as you can get. Here are my rules, says YHWH. Do it my way or *boom!*

John 2:13-25 is more complex, if less elegant, but the overriding impression is of Jesus laying down the Law.

Like Father, like Son.

To be fair, Jesus is not being presented here so much as the divine Son of God as the messiah, the liberator of Israel. As he cleanses the temple, his followers think of Psalm 69 ("Zeal for your house consumes me"), a lamentation Psalm commonly recited at the time in a messianic context. But the emotions and behavior of the messiah mirror the emotions and behavior of YHWH.

These are angry, jealous denizens of the Middle East. You can almost see the fists being raised and the rocks being tossed in the background.

Western Christians are uncomfortable with these images. American gods may be tough on foreign devils, but they are tender with the home crowd. They do not grab us by the throat and order us to do things. Nobody does (and gets away with it).

So the American God is nice, gentle, and democratic. Jesus is the same. Americans have rejected, in many ways, the rough-hewn God of Hebrew scripture who laid down the Law with so much passion and have created, with some pride, a passionless God of unconditional love.

This shift is seen as a development—sometimes psychological (from a judgmental father-god of childhood to a loving god of adulthood), sometimes scriptural (from the warlike God of the "Old" Testament to the pacific Jesus of the "New" Testament).

Today's combination of readings challenges this view. Jesus here is a chip off a very old, jealous, angry, loving block. There are, if not conditions to God's love, at least terrible consequences for not accepting it.

God's love is like the love of a real parent. In the real world, a parent's love is not "unconditional" in the sense that the child can do anything while the parent smiles lovingly and says "ain't she sweet." A parent's love is an intense, demanding (especially at certain stages), everlasting kind of love that can go through a full range of emotions. Including anger. Including threatening to ground the recalcitrant child for three or four generations. But the parent's love, translated in Hebrew as *chesed* and in Greek as *agape*, is always there.

But you don't want to mess with it.

Y'Shua: The Tricky Messiah

Occasion: *12th Sunday of the Year (B)*

א

> "There is neither Jew nor Greek, there is neither slave nor free person, there is not male and female; ...all are one in Christ Jesus." (Gal 3:28)

"**W**hy don't we become Jewish?" my minister-friend and fellow traveler said after a little too much of the broth.

"Do you believe in Jesus Christ, the only Son, who was crucified, died, and was buried on the third day?" I said.

"Oh," he said. "That."

That. The most liberal rabbis frown on would-be converts who cannot shake the idea of the incarnation worked out in the life of a man named Jesus. So neither of us has become Jewish, but the pull remains and seems to be growing stronger. Often I am more comfortable in Jewish places than in Christian ones. I can no longer pass up celebrating Passover at home, but I am perfectly willing to miss a leg or two of the Triduum. The intense, ethical debates at the local conservative synagogue touch something deeper in me than my pastor's simpler insistence on God's unconditional love. And any talk of developing a personal relationship with Jesus makes me squirm.

29

So how is it that I find myself editing a magazine for Christian professionals? How is it that I find myself more involved than ever in my parish? Why, for heaven's sake, do I find myself involved in evangelism? Why, for Christ's sake, do people seem to look to me when they are thinking of coming into or back to the church?

I don't know the answer to that one—except the usual observation that God works in mysterious ways. But I have had to try to make peace between the Judaism and Christianity that battle within my soul.

Part of the solution, of course, is to recognize the common roots of Judaism and Christianity. Jesus has grown on me precisely to the extent that I have learned to see him as Y'Shua, an incredible presence who echoes Moses, Elijah, the prophets, the Suffering Servant, and the embodiment of the spirit of Torah. But that is not enough. If the Jesus of history seems to embody Judaism, the Jesus of the Resurrection seems to separate Jews from Greeks. Contrary to what St. Paul said and hoped, in Christ, there are Jews and there are Greeks, there are non-believers and there are believers. And they are painfully separate, to the point of murder in Christ's name.

The possibility of St. Paul's phrase—"There is neither Jew nor Greek ... for in Christ you are one"—comes to reality, I believe, only when the paschal mystery is acted out. That is, Christ must die in order to rise.

This is not exactly a shocking thought, but what the Christian community often misses is that this process is constant. Christ is *always* dying in order to be *always* rising.

For example, there is a tradition that Christ appears in the guise of a beggar. Christ dies to the image of the triumphant, resurrected Christ and reappears again in lowly and not necessarily attractive human form. Christ is always dying to the expected and rising in unexpected places. In Gospel time, things are never what they appear to be. The rich become poor, the poor become rich; life becomes death, death becomes life.

Similarly, evangelism is most effective when it is coyote tricky. Mike Moynahan, the Jesuit dramatist, says that good religious drama does not necessarily retell the Gospel in a recognizable way. Indeed, the recognizability of a story may prevent someone from hearing its message. The very name of Christ may not be mentioned—indeed cannot be mentioned in some cases—or the message will be closed off.

An orthodox rabbi, when asked by a Christian student what would happen at the end of the world, said: "I think you will see the Christ and I will see the Messiah."

It would be so like him.

The Mighty Mustard Bush

Occasion: *11th Sunday of the Year (B)*

א

I had a chance to see Bishop Kenneth Untener of Saginaw, MI, give one of his overhead-projector performances.

He is a very funny man and, not incidentally, a wise one with the ability to use pictures to make obvious what was once obscure.

In this particular "keynote address," for example, he said that our image of church was changing from an ancient institution to a very young, immature one.

Often we imagine the church as a tree, he said, flashing on the screen a reasonable resemblance to a hoary oak. Ah, yes, the picture of the church as a solid, if stodgy, institution flashes through the mind.

The church may be a tree, he said, but is it an old tree?

To make the point, he switched metaphors and flashed on the screen a picture that represented the history of the church in relationship to the history of the world. Thousands of tiny fish in neat little rows were followed by one tiny fish in a different color. That was the church, a rather young thing in the history of the world, immature and childlike.

Given the picture, his point seems obvious, but I know we still apply our old images of church to the Gospel.

Take the story of the mustard seed that grows up into "the greatest of all trees."

How often have you heard the story? How often have you told it?

Read it again (Mt 13:31-32; Mk 4:30-32; Lk 13:19), with a cross-check to a field guide to wild flowers or a spring walk in a meadow. The mustard seed is not the smallest of all seeds. Nor is the "tree," even assuming Jesus is referring to the perennial shrub instead of the common annual, more than ten feet tall.

Jesus is playing with his listeners' minds here. The normal metaphor for a grand idea like the "realm of God" would have been the cedar of Lebanon. In fact, the reference in the Gospel to the birds of the air who and dwell in the shade of the mustard bush mimics a reference to a "majestic cedar" from the first reading from this Sunday. (Ez 17:22-24)

The cedar, in Daniel 4:21, reaches up to the heavens and is visible throughout the whole earth.

The mighty mustard bush is nothing so grand.

It is not, mind you, a horrible plant. In the spring, when mustard flowers cover the hills and orchards of Galilee as they do here in California, a community of mustard plants is even breathtaking. A wild, colorful, whimsical sign of the earth's renewal.

Not a bad symbol for the church when you think about it.

Part III:
Feasts and Seasons

No Room In What Inn?

Occasion: *Christmas*
א

The picture sticks in my mind of an innkeeper, door cracked, telling an obviously pregnant young woman and her much-older husband to go away because the inn is full.

It goes along with other childhood images of the Christmas story: A very holy Mary with her arms crossed peculiarly over her breast while listening to the angel Gabriel; Joseph, staff in hand, leading a donkey atop of which sleeps a tired and pregnant wife; a kindly old man who offers to let the young couple sleep in the barn; and, of course, the stable.

The innkeeper picture bothers me most of all. The image is vivid and anti-semitic. He has a hooked nose and beady eyes. He is at best preoccupied with his own problems, and at worst a greedy Shylock who worries that an untimely birth will drive away his paying guests.

That's a lot of image for a man who isn't even in the original story.

We aren't as obviously anti-semitic these days, but even the best preaching seems to lock on the idea that the Christmas story is a tale of rejection. Poor outcast baby, born in a barn, because there was no room in the the inn.

The interpretation comes from Luke 2:7: "...and she gave birth to her firstborn son. She wrapped him in swaddling clothes and laid him in a manger, because there was no room for them in the inn."

The Greek word translated here as "inn" is *katalyma*, which actually means a room for a guest or for eating. The original translation of the New American Bible translated katalyma with the accurate but cumbersome "place where travelers lodged." There were no Holiday Inns or Motel 6's in small villages like Bethlehem. Abrahamic hospitality provided. In normal times, strangers who entered the village sat in the *saha* (open space or commons) until the first villager came by and offered the hospitality of his home; not to do so would have brought shame on the entire community. But Joseph was not a stranger. Bethlehem was his ancestral home and he would have stayed with relatives.

Granted that a census, if there were such and event, would have strained the capacity of the town to offer normal hospitality. But that is the point. Joseph and Mary were provided for—even though the guestroom was full.

How do we know?

By the manger. Today, we are used to animals being kept in separate barns. But in first-century Palestine, animals were kept inside the homes, in rooms open and adjacent to the main living room. The feeding troughs—the mangers—sat between the main living area and the animal quarters.

Far from being isolated in a remote barn, Jesus—according to Luke's story—spent his first days being cooed over by his mother and father, animals, and other relatives (we may guess), shepherds, and representatives of the prophetic community (Simeon and Anna).

I have a friend who thinks that Simeon's messianic prophecy ("Behold, this child is destined for the fall and rise of many in Israel" — Lk 2:34) was nothing more than an old man telling proud parents that their boy was going to grow up to be president someday. Luke probably had more on his mind, but my friend's interpretation suggests at least that what is most extraordinary about the Christmas story is its ordinariness. A child was born, people gathered round, brought gifts, heaped praise on the new prodigy, and made goo-goo noises.

Welcome to the incarnation.

Still, homilists and parents will fix on the non-existent innkeeper peering out from behind his triple-locked door. Let that interpretation remind us of the wound that has existed between Jew and Greek since the time of St. Paul and of the need, this Christmas, to be more like those ordinary Jews who found a way of making room for a newborn boy in the midst of their crowded lives.

Mothers of the Messiah

As many as two churches in the United States will read the long form of the Gospel (Mt 1:1-25) for Christmas midnight Mass.

My lector's notes suggest that making the proclamation interesting is a lost cause and that the best the lector can do is read the passage without stumbling over the names. Nothing like a little pep talk.

Granted, Amminadab, Shealtiel, and Zerubbabel don't fall trippingly off the tongue, but this portion is more fun that it appears to be.

Matthew's genealogy is composed of three sections of fourteen names (two times the sacred number, seven), including those of five women. This is significant because legal rights at the time passed only through the father.

Moreover, each of the women had a moral flaw connected with sex.

Tamar pretended to be a temple prostitute and seduced Judah, her father-in-law, getting twins by him. (Gn 38)

Rahab was a Canaanite prostitute. (Jos 2)

Ruth sneaked into Boaz' bed and induced him to marry her. (Ru 3)

Bathsheba, Uriah's wife, committed adultery with David during the time of her uncleanness and married him after David arranged for her husband's death in battle. (2 Sam 11)

Mary was found to be with child before marriage. (Mt 1:18)

Since the purpose of the genealogy was to connect Jesus with Abraham and to establish him as the messiah, one might have expected Matthew, if he were going to mention any women at all, to mention more conventional mothers of the messiah like Sarah, Rebekkah, Rachel, or Leah.

He does not.

In *Biblical Affirmations of Women* (Westminster Press, 1979), Leonard Swidler suggests that Matthew's list was meant to counteract claims that Jesus could not be the messiah because his origins were extramarital and therefore "immoral." Instead of denying the stories, Matthew included in his genealogy other sexually irregular women who played key roles in Israel's history.

Tamar was associated with the founding fathers of the twelve tribes of Israel and, in her sexually irregular way, was "more righteous" than Judah. Rahab aided the Israelite army and helped win the promised land. Ruth, another non-Jew, showed remarkable fidelity to the God of Israel and was remembered as a founding mother of the House of Israel. Bathsheba, wife of Uriah, was also wife to Israel's first real king and mother of Solomon.

Curiously, Bathsheba is not mentioned by name and is instead referred to as the woman "who had been married to Uriah." Perhaps Matthew thought her sin deserved namelessness, but more likely, he deliberately mentioned Uriah to call attention to the adultery and murder for a Jewish audience that grew up on this ancient version of *Dynasty*.

The genealogy is context for the story of a young maiden who one day wakes up pregnant and is almost put away by her righteous spouse. The wondrous story of the angel overlays a scandal: Mary was caught in the appearance of adultery.

God works in mysterious ways. Those who seem to be unholy are holy. Those who seem to be last are first. That things are not what they seem to be is the point of the genealogy and the story of Mary and the life of her famous offspring.

Beginning with a Blessing

Occasion: *New Year's Day*
א

You know you're in trouble liturgically when a holy day has several different names, none of which seem to be related. On January 1, the Roman calendar has variously celebrated the feast of the circumcision of Jesus (oh boy); the solemnity of Mary, the Mother of God; World Day of Peace; and the Octave of Christmas. The Common Lectionary, using the same readings, would add the Holy Name of Jesus and, with different readings entirely, New Year's Day. And, of course, the weight of the culture is with New Year's Day.

No matter what feast-name you choose, this is one occasion when the New Testament readings are read most easily as commentaries on a more primary reading from Hebrew scriptures.

The Aaronic blessing (Nm 6:22-27) re-emphasized in the Psalm responsorial (Ps 67), is a lovely way to begin a new year. The blessing contains an early hint of God as loving father. "The Lord let his face shine upon you" is poetry for a smile. And the prayer for "peace" is a prayer for "shalom," which contains within it those rich Middle Eastern images of prosperity, fertility, and contentment. Exactly what one would wish for one's dearest friends at the beginning of the year.

Questions arise about the reading, however. Why did God tell Moses to tell Aaron to give the blessing? Why did God not give the blessing directly or at least tell Moses to give it? For some reason, this blessing must be filtered through Moses (the Law) and again through Aaron (the liturgy). Prosperity comes in faithfulness to the covenant and in gathering together as a people for worship. It is not to happen, willy-nilly, automatically.

What do the New Testament readings have to say about this?

In this case it is helpful to look at the Gospel (Lk 2:16-21) first because it is the less radical of the two. The first part of the story contains the message that God's blessing goes out through Jesus to the shepherds. The shepherd image is ambivalent: key Jewish heroes like Abraham and David were shepherds, but shepherds were also perceived in the culture as low-class, suspicious characters prone to thievery. Everyone was "astonished" by their story because no one could believe a shepherd. The Gospel is probably picking up on this image to extend the blessing of the covenant, through Christ, to those on the margin of the nation of Israel. The second part of the story, the reference to Jesus' circumcision, "baptizes" the story as a Jewish one. Jesus is a Jew and the blessing that is being passed on to these shepherds and their ilk is the blessing of the covenant.

The second reading (Gal 4:4-7) is the tough one. Although circumcision is not mentioned here, the passage occurs in the context of a polemic against Judaizing Christians who insisted on circumcision and other Jewish practices for gentile Christians. Paul insists that the gentile Christians are "adopted" children of God and rightful heirs to the blessings of the covenant.

In the letter, Paul clearly argues that the blessing, which used to pass through the Law and the liturgy, now passes through Christ. However, be careful about reading Paul's letter as evidence that Christians are the *only* heirs to the blessing of the covenant. We are "adopted" sons and daughters, entitled therefore to the blessing, but we do not displace the firstborn child any more than the prodigal son displaced his older brother.

Hosanna!
Liberate Us Now!

Occasion: *Palm Sunday*
א

One day, as I explained to some eleven-year-olds that *hosanna* meant "free us," I saw a skeptical eyebrow raise.

"Free us in the highest?" asked the eyebrow owner rhetorically.

"Very good," I said lamely. "You remember the 'Holy, Holy, Holy' from the Mass."

Meantime, I tried to figure out if it was worth telling this kid that her church has been invincibly ignorant of Hebrew approximately since Peter caved into Paul. Very early in the game, Christians quit studying things Jewish, including the language, so that by the second century pious Christian scribes figured any foreign sounding word must mean "Praise the Lord!" and deserved to be embellished with "in the highest." At least they got *Alleluia* right.

Hosanna, for the record, is Hebrew for "Free us!" or "Save us!" or "Liberate us!" or "Help!"—although one liturgist I know says that 1,800-plus years of usage makes it mean "Praise the Lord" and Today's English Version of the Bible actually translates the hosanna of the triumphal entry into Jerusalem as "Praise!"

Sigh. I am holding out for the original meaning with what I hope is more than a linguistic quibble.

For starters, Jesus' name (Hebrew: *yehoshuah*) means "Yahweh saves" and comes from the same root as hosanna.

Secondly, hosanna as liberation is fundamental to an understanding of the triumphal entry into Jerusalem.

If you think the crowd was saying "praise" to a gentle man on a donkey, that is one thing.

If you think the crowd was saying "liberate us" to the conquering messiah, it is quite another.

I'm going with the latter. For three thousand years, Jews have been celebrating the fall harvest of *sukkot* by marching around their places of worship while shouting "Hosanna!" and beating palm branches. No one is quite sure about the palm branches — except that the action is clearly evocative — but the hosanna is clearly a cry of liberation, as old as Moses and as recent as the state of Israel. Today, the Sukkot processions occur in synagogues. In Jesus' time, they occurred on the temple grounds. Jesus' entry into Jerusalem may have took place during Sukkot, in the fall rather than the spring; certainly the event evoked Sukkot symbols for his Jewish followers.

Matthew's reference to a text from Zechariah ("Behold, your king comes to you, meek and riding on an ass... ") gives a gentler, humbler cast to the event than it may have had. (Mt 21:5) The donkey may have been a symbol of humility in Zechariah's time, but in Jesus' time it was the mount of choice for a Roman general. So here was a Galilean Jew with messianic pretensions riding into a Roman-ruled city, riding a general's mount, riding over cloaks that people spread before royalty—while the Jews shout "Liberate us!" The impact would be roughly equivalent to Yasser Araphat riding an open jeep into Old Jerusalem while the Arab population shouts "Liberate us! Save us! Free us!" The authorities would notice.

So when I say the "Holy, Holy, Holy, Lord God of Hosts," I remember that "hosts" originally meant an army and that the one who comes "in the name of the Lord," is the messiah. The conquering king. Alleluia comes after liberation. Palm Sunday before Easter. Hosanna! Liberate us! Save us! Free us!

Footwashing as Eucharist

Occasion: *Holy Thursday*
א

S ome rituals, like some words, lose meaning in
the translation. Footwashing, for example.

The standard lesson received, if you're watching
the pope wash the feet of a peasant or Jimmy Carter
wash the feet of a Republican, is one of humility.
Sometimes, though, humility is on the the other
foot; I was always embarrassed to have my one foot
washed in public and always made sure I had
bathed well before, which, when you think about it,
removes the ceremony one more step from reality.

But humility is only incidental to the original
point, which had to do with hospitality. Consider:

Abraham, venerated as the father of hospitality in
semitic religions, offers first a footbath and then a
meal to the strangers who appear to him under the
oaks of Mamre. (Gn 18) He bows deeply, as was the
custom, and speaks humbly: "Sir, if I may ask you
this favor, please do not go on past your servant."
(Gn 18:3). This is the florid language of the Bedouin
host-as-servant.

One chapter later, Lot uses similar language to
offer the strangers (now two) lodging and then a
footbath.

In John 12 and Luke 7, Jesus accepts a footbath of
tears from a woman and scolds his host for not
providing the customary water.

And in the passage read from John's Gospel on Holy Thursday night, Jesus-as-host washes the feet of his guests. Curiously, this is the only ritual action mentioned in John's account of the Last Supper.

People who no longer wash even their hands before a meal can be forgiven for not quite getting the drift of these stories, but it is worth asking why the footbath was so important.

Sanitation, surely, but the custom does not seem to have its origins in the city whose pavements are infinitely nastier than the soil of the countryside. Neither the big-city Sodomites nor Simon, the city pharisee, nor even (in John's account) Jesus' good friend Lazarus offers the hospitality of the footbath. That is left to the nomads Abraham and Lot, women, and a small-town boy from Galilee.

There are clues there. Nomads, even though they live in tents, establish a marked difference between inside and outside through ritual and rugs. The wise host did not let his guests drag sheep poop and sand all over the wife's oriental rugs; hence the removal of shoes and the washing of the feet. The ritual, in turn, makes a transition between outside and inside, where "outside" represents danger and "inside" represents safety and intimacy. Bedouin hospitality is more than the sharing of vittles; it is an offer of protection, a pledge to shed blood, if necessary, to defend the life of the guest.

Thus, Lot pledges his own blood (his daughters) to protect the blood of his guests, and Jesus pledges his own blood to protect (in Hebrew, the same word applies for "defend," "save," and "liberate") his guests.

The breaking of bread, the sharing of the cup, the pledging of blood, the washing of feet, are the same

symbol. And Jesus, like many revolutionaries, is
calling his followers to what is best and deepest in
their own tradition.

Embracing
the Absence of God

Occasion: *Good Friday*
א

W e didn't know how to do a lot of things well
twenty-five years ago, but by golly we did a good
Good Friday. Removing the Eucharist, stripping the
altar, snuffing the lamp, and throwing the
tabernacle door open at the end of the Holy
Thursday service *worked*. We had lots of linens and
gee-gaws around the altar in those days and a
tabernacle that was the center of attention. Stripping
was sad. An unspeakable symbol of emptiness. You
could *feel* the absence of God, the dislocation of
walking into a church and wanting to genuflect, but
to what? For one time a year, there was nothing
there. Nothing to pay homage to. Nothing but the
cross and the unspeakable emptiness of the God
who died. The warm blood of the Eucharist replaced
by the brittle sound of the Word. And only the Word.

Good Friday doesn't work as well any more. The
tabernacle, in our renovated church, is permanently
out of sight. The linens are minimal to begin with.
The design is plain. Stripping it for Good Friday
would leave a church that looks like Ordinary Time.
Yet Good Friday is not Ordinary Time, which is full
of the ordinary goodness of God. Good Friday is
extraordinary; it is empty and dead.

Liturgists are in the business of filling space and time. On this day—the holiest of the year in its way—it is best to do nothing. On a normal day, we eat; on this day, we fast. On a normal day, we sing; on this day, we are silent; on a normal day, we gather in community; on this day, we are into ourselves. The assembly, our modern tabernacle, is thrown open and gazes at its own emptiness and *feels* the absence of God.

This is not easy. The point of worship, usually, is to feel the presence of God and to touch the mystery. Reasonable human beings do not try to feel the ache of nothing. They instinctively will go to the symbol of the presence if you let them.

My home parish used to reserve the Eucharist on Good Friday on a side altar, which was dressed to the nines for the occasion by the ladies of the Altar Guild. Naturally, parishioners would enter the church, ignore the large wooden cross, and make a beeline for the highly visible eucharistic chapel and make a great show of genuflecting on both knees. This is too bad. Good Friday is a set-up for Easter, but the fullness of the Easter experience comes only after the fullness of the Good Friday experience. To reach Easter one has to first cry out in the despair of the psalmist and Jesus: "My God, My God, why have you forsaken me?" (Ps 22:1)

Groping for God

Occasion: *Third Sunday of Easter (B)*

א

"**T**ouch me!" the risen Jesus says at the end of Luke's Gospel. (Lk 24:39)

Throughout the Gospels Jesus touches and is touched. In all those passages, the Greek word is *hapto*, which connotes a kindling of the fire from his healing hand. This time, though, the word is *pselephao* and it comes up in the Gospels just this once. "Touch" does not convey the full sense of *pselephao*, which is the word you would use to describe how a blind person touches someone's face to "see" them. It is used in three other places—twice to refer to this passage and once to describe how humans were to "seek God, even perhaps *grope for* him and find him." (Acts 17:27)

The demand belongs to mystagogia. It comes up twice in the Roman Lectionary, first implicitly with Jesus' demand that Thomas put his hand into Jesus side (Jn 20:27, second week of Easter) and again a week later with the *pselephao* in Luke's passage. "Touch me" is a demand to come to terms with the Resurrection through one's own whole being — physical, emotional, mental, and spiritual. Mystagogia is no head trip.

Yet that is precisely the danger. Early Christians, like their modern cousins, were apt to whiz off into the clouds—especially when talking about something as potentially fuzzy as the Resurrection.

The storyteller clearly intends to prove that Jesus is no ghost, no phantom, no spirit, no *pneuma*. The author of Luke-Acts is making a distinction between this experience (confronting Jesus as not-spirit) and the experience at Pentecost (confronting the Spirit). Curiously, the body-before-us is not as easy to believe as the Spirit-we-cannot-see. People will believe in spiritualities, in ghosts and phantoms and philosophies, but not in what they can touch or in who they can touch. And yet, in Matthew 25, it is clear that the risen Christ is found in who is touched.

You can feel the resistance to touching in the story. In John, Jesus tells Thomas to stick his hand into his wound. This is meant to be challenging and even gross. The command is unsettling and a bit reminiscent of Jesus' own practice of touching the wounds and sores of the many people he healed. Here he is asking for a turnabout, as if he has now taken the place of all those lepers. It is not meant to be easy. If it were, Thomas might have touched the wound instead of uttering a prayer.

A Jew could not touch a wound—or the dead—without becoming unclean. Such purification rules identified the community, kept it clean, and held it together. But the messianic message linked the clean and the unclean and forged a new community.

In the end, the new Christian will grope for the messiah and find him in the bodiliness of the outcast. The Spirit, this *pneuma*, drives the neophyte into this awful contact. In a beautiful post-Pentecost story, Peter and John confront a crippled panhandler, look him in the eye, grasp him and and yank him to his feet in the name of Jesus Christ. The beggar dances for joy and "clings to" Peter and John.

This is the community of the messiah. Someday, after conversion, after mystagogia, I might even be able to do the same.

Drunken Butterflies

No wonder mystagogia is the murkiest period of the RCIA process. It comes during the murkiest, least understandable portion of the liturgical year.

Think about it. Advent and Christmas, no problem. Ordinary time, a breather. No problem. Lent and Holy Week, no problem. The Triduum, great. It all makes sense in a rhythmical, deep-down, catholic human sort of way.

But Easter-as-fifty-days, Ascension, Pentecost? Problems. See, you can do forty days of discipline, but can you do fifty days of feast? You practice and practice and practice and when you finally play the game, it's over in an hour. Not even the Christmas season, where we eat and party till we pop, lasts for fifty days. The culture wants it over on the 26th, just for some relief.

The problem may be that Easter is both a catharsis and something of a puzzlement, both an event and a process.

Think of the old butterfly analogy. Usually, people see the transformation of the caterpillar to a butterfly as a metaphor for what happens between Good Friday and Easter morning. Thus, Easter morning is the moment the butterfly emerges from the cocoon. Used in this way, the metaphor focuses on the event because there is not much, nothing really, that happens between Good Friday and Easter. The cocoon as dead tomb.

In reality, though, the transformation of the caterpillar into a butterfly is a titanic birthing process that involves incredible struggle, struggle I'm told that is necessary for the butterfly to mature correctly.

The cocoon metaphor can also be applied to what happens to the followers of Jesus between the empty tomb experience and their empowerment by the Holy Spirit. Here, you have to see Easter as a process that takes this community from fear and horror (belief that Jesus' body had been stolen) to a sense that he was somehow among them—here again and gone again—to a sense of power, a sense that *they* were the messiah in the world.

I am told that something like this process can happen to people involved in 12-step fellowships like Alcoholics Anonymous, Al Anon, or Overeater's Anonymous. Initially, people are miserable, full of fear and terror; then there is a period of euphoria and hope, followed by more complex feelings as they set about to work on their problems. One step, the eleventh, sounds suspiciously similar to what the followers of Jesus might have been experiencing in the upper room after watching the Ascension: "Sought through prayer and meditation to improve our conscious contact with God as we understood him, praying only for knowledge of his will for us and the power to carry that out."

Even people who have had a life-changing experience are reluctant to get out into the world and behave in unfamiliar ways. Therefore one needs to pray for the knowledge of what to do and, especially, the power to do it.

After that, for apostles and alcoholics, for butterflies and neophytes, it's out into the world.

The funny thing is, when the apostles got the power and left the upper room, everyone thought they were drunk.

Babble On

The Tower of Babel story (Gn 11) comes up as an alternate reading for Pentecost in the Common Lectionary and as the first reading for the Vigil in the Roman Lectionary. On the face of it, the Tower of Babel story seems almost the flip side of the Pentecost story itself. (Acts 2)

Compare first the similarities:

Both have to do with language (and cultural) differences.

Both are set in great cosmopolitan centers: Babylon and Jerusalem.

Both are stories about how God descends on a people in a dramatic way.

Now the differences:

In Genesis, the movement is from unity to disunity; in Acts, the movement is from disunity to unity. Babel begins with a common language and ends in "babble"; Jerusalem begins in "babble" and ends in understanding.

Genesis emphasizes the downfall of the lofty Babylonians; Acts emphasizes the rise of the humble Galileans.

In Genesis, the Lord is the creator of discord; in Acts, the Spirit is the creator of harmony.

This last point suggests that there is more going on here than nice stories. In fact, the Lord comes off as

60

anything but a nice guy. Or, I should say, nice *guys*; Genesis 11 is one of three places where the divine pronoun is plural. (One of the other places [Gn 3:22] also happens to show the Lord fretting that human beings will become like "us.")

Says the Lord: "If now, while they are one people, all speaking the same language, they have started to do this, nothing will later stop them from doing what they presume to do. Let us then go down and there confuse their language, so that one will not understand what another says." (Gn 11)

Say what you want about the need for humans to stay humble, but this makes the Lord sound more like Ferdinand Marcos than Jesus of Nazareth. "Come, the people may go all the way. Let us go down and stuff the ballot boxes."

This is the dark side of God. Fearful. Divisive. Disruptive. Yet it is only one side of the same coin. Look again at the Acts story, where the Spirit appears on the surface as a creative force bringing harmony to a new Jerusalem, and you will see the darkness. The spirit comes in the violence of wind and fire, destroying old lives, bewildering the masses. "They have had too much new wine," say bystanders, further confusing normal categories, for "babblers" now communicate and the sober do not.

And now look at the light side of Babel, whose destruction sent us off on the rich road to cultural and linguistic pluralism. The Pentecost Spirit did not change that direction; it only enabled us to "hear" in our own language, even as it added more tongues, more gifts, and more richness.

Sacrament of Gifts

Occasion: *Pentecost*

א

One evening, while explaining the sacraments to a group of returning Catholics, the pastor sighed and admitted that Confirmation is a sacrament in search of theology. "But it's really about receiving the gifts of the Spirit."

Click.

He went onto the next sacrament. But I kept thinking about that click. Heretofore, I had thought that Confirmation celebrated one's commitment to Jesus Christ. Of course, that understanding creates endless confusion because Baptism—at least for adults—is a celebration of one's commitment to Jesus Christ. With the same understanding of Confirmation, one comes inevitably to the conclusion that Baptism and Confirmation are really part of the same sacrament and should be celebrated together, which raises more questions than it answers. Especially if you think that good things come in sevens.

But the pastor's definition had the promise of clarity, assuming I could get a handle on what was meant by "gifts of the Spirit." I vaguely recalled a list of seven from the Baltimore Catechism and knew that charismatics talked about receiving the gifts at the "Baptism of the Spirit." Were we talking about seven specific gifts? Were we talking about charismatic gifts? Something told me no. A quick reading of 1 Corinthians 12 told me why. St. Paul appears to be listing, somewhat informally, the various talents found in the Corinthian church. His point is that there are "different kinds of spiritual gifts but the same Spirit," not that there are seven distinct gifts of the Spirit. When writing to the Romans, Paul makes a longer and less charismatic list of gifts. (Rom 12) In writing to both, he was probably listing the individual strengths he found in each church. In both places, he is telling his people that individual talents can all be used to serve the Lord. Different strokes for different folks.

What does it mean if we agree that Confirmation is about celebrating the reception of the gifts of the Spirit? Surely it does not mean celebrating the reception of seven specific charismatic gifts—although this might work in a highly charged charismatic community. But in the average parish, few people receive any charismatic gifts, let alone all of them. Yet in every parish, there are a significant number of people who have found their talent, their gift, and who are using it in service to the Lord. There are, to be sure, many others who are more passive. They believe, they come, but they contribute relatively little.

Is not this passage from believer to active contributor what is celebrated in the sacrament of Confirmation? Is this not comparable to the transition that is made from the first Easter Sunday, when the reality of the risen Lord first breaks upon the community, to Pentecost, when that community finds its throat and moves out into the world?

And if this is an apt comparison, why do we insist on confirming neophytes immediately after Baptism? The liturgical year has built in a period of struggle between Easter and Pentecost. Does not this same struggle exist in the human psyche? First I believe, then I find out how I can contribute.

This model suggests a clear mission for the mystagogic stage of the catechumenal process. The task is to help the neophytes find their special gifts and show them how to incorporate them into the community. Confirmation, on Pentecost, then becomes a celebration of all those individual gifts coming together in service to the Lord. This in-gathering, of the gifts rather than the nations, fits with the original harvest character of Jewish Pentecost.

If you understand Confirmation as a celebration of the reception of the gifts of the Spirit, you will also know when it is appropriate to confirm someone. Certainly not in infancy. Not in childhood. And probably not in adolescence. This is a sacrament of maturity, celebrated with those who have found out who they are in the context of the church.

Take My Cup...Please!

Occasion: *Corpus Christi*
ℵ

The common cup may be the single most powerful symbol in the liturgy.

You can tell because so many refuse to drink from it. On any given Sunday, when the cup is offered, maybe a third of the congregation will accept. These are not only, or even mostly, people who reject the tenets of Vatican II. These are people who should know better. Once, during an RCIA session, I wanted to pass around an agape cup. The team leader objected because it was flu season.

The phenomenon reminds me of those pre-Vatican II days when only a minority of people went to Communion. Then, people held back out of a sense of sinfulness; now, I fear, people hold back out of fear of commitment. If Baptism represents the neophyte's initial immersion into the community, drinking from the common cup represents the continuation of the Christian's willingness to drink deeply from the community's experience. The good news, I suppose, is that most people sense that drinking deeply is serious business—and simply refuse to do it.

Christian scriptures refer to the cup in similar ways on three different occasions:

Once Jesus asks the apostles, "Can you drink the cup that I am going to drink?" (Mt 20:22)

Again, when Jesus "took a cup, gave thanks, and gave it to them saying, 'Drink from it, all of you, for this is my blood of the covenant, which will be shed....' " (Mt 26:27-28)

And again when Jesus asks his father to "let this cup pass from me." (Mt 26:39)

This use of "cup" in the New Testament seems consistent with the Hebrew scriptures where the cup is variously "the cup of salvation" (Ps 116:13); "the cup of his wrath" (Is 51:17); "the cup of consolation" (Jer 16:7); "a cup of dismay." (Ez 23:33)

Each time, "the cup" is a metaphor for the totality of an experience. The cup is the container of the experience; to drink from the cup is to pass from spectator to participant and to become one with the experience—a daunting thought when the experience involves suffering and death.

Drinking from this cup is not a casual act and springs from an adult experience of suffering and ordeal rather than the more childlike experience of sitting at table with mommy and daddy.

I like to point out that sharing the cup is an ancient Middle Eastern custom used on many occasions—and carried the weight of a pledge to shed one's own blood for whomever shared the cup with you. Once Lot shared the cup with the two strangers, he was bound to protect them more than his own blood (his daughters). Once a soldier drank from the common cup, he was duty bound to shed his blood for his fellows. Hospitality runs deeper than coffee and doughnuts—as sanctuary churches know.

The refuseniks know it too. The common cup contains our worst fears of what it means to be community. If you get too close, you get sick—and maybe die. Liturgists can say all they want about AIDS not being passed on through a common cup, but those who fear the worst have at least understood the symbol. If you get too close, you suffer—and maybe die. That is the point.

You can look at this way. Bread is the softer symbol of the Eucharist: homey, wholesome, enriching, inviting, available to everyone, a symbol of life. Wine is the harder symbol: red, bloody, spirited, transformative, dangerous, limited, sacrificial, a symbol of death.

Until recently, I thought we should discontinue offering the common cup at large assemblies—since logistically and psychologically the cup seems to work best in small groups. Today I think the common cup, passed up by two-thirds of a large assembly, serves as an important reminder that real community and real intimacy is not as easy as distributing a few wafers of bread.

Gleaning and Justice

Occasion: *Autumn*
א

The worst part of teaching sixth-grade CCD—aside from showing up on the first day—was knowing that we (which is to say, I) were responsible for the first monthly children's Mass of the school year.

Not that I minded planning a liturgy. It is just that good Masses come out of communities—and the possibility of any sixth grade being a community after five or so one-and-a-half-hour CCD sessions was dim.

I needed to build community — fast. Armed with advice from two friends—one interested in Judaism and the other in outdoor education—I devised two projects that were successful enough to repeat in two subsequent years.

One was building a *sukkah*, a shelter (booth or tabernacle) built during the feast of *sukkot* as a reminder of the time the Israelites lived in temporary shelters on the Sinai and of the harvest (see "Playing with Fire," page 83). Fieldworkers customarily slept under these shelters during the harvest instead of returning every night to their villages. A sukkah is supposed to be built with a roof that is open to the stars, but in the first year we installed ours—composed of privet branches and boughs—in a room that used to serve as a library. Weird, and not exactly kosher, but an attention-grabber. The novelty and difficulty of the task helped give the class some early identity. To keep the custom of using the sukkah for meal sharing, eighteen of us gathered underneath and shared popcorn.

The second project was gleaning a cornfield. In rural Illinois, 4-H clubs and the like occasionally gleaned fields as a way of raising money, but our farmers were not in touch with the biblical origins of the custom: "When you reap the harvest of your land, you shall not be so thorough that you reap the field to its very edge, nor shall you glean the stray ears of grain...These things you shall leave them for the poor and the alien. I am the LORD..." (Lv 19:9-10)

Gleaning is a magnificent, if virtually unused, system of providing for the poor out of every harvest while allowing them the dignity of their own labor. Gleaning with kids is not exactly what the Mosaic Code had in mind, but I recommend it anyway. It is a memorable, community-building activity (especially when done in the biting October wind) that connects religion and nature for both young people and adults alike. The actual gleaning was done by the kids and two teachers. To touch the rest of the community, we used liturgy.

Incorporating gleaning into the liturgy was simple. All it took was corn, carried up to the altar in bushels. Farmers suddenly knew that the work of their hands, their harvest, was the work of the Lord. An unexpected connection occurred when the kids placed their offerings off to the side, underneath the statue of the Blessed Mother, which, in our church, had been carved in a Native American style. Images of grain and maize, blessed mother and fertility goddess, seemed to run together. We were involved in very ancient rites here.

Yet we are not merely fertility worshippers. YHWH is a God of nature *and* justice. Just as the sukkah celebrates both the harvest and liberation from slavery, gleaning is both harvest and justice-making.

So part of the process for the sixth grade each year was deciding how to spend their corn money—and throwing a pizza party for themselves wasn't allowed. They could, however, throw a pizza party for the second grade and take bouquets of roses to residents at the local nursing home. And that's what they did.

Harvest and Liberation

Occasion: *All Saints*
א

Holy days ought to be festivals. Indeed, I
imagine at one time they were. But by my lifetime,
holy days had degenerated into "days of obligation"
when one attended a perfunctory liturgy as a kind of
grudging duty. Today, with less emphasis on
obligation and no more emphasis on festivity, U.S.
holy days are even more vestigial.

Yet the feast of All Saints, tied as it is to the
culturally popular Halloween, could become a great
liturgical festival if communities paid attention.
Clues as to how to celebrate this seemingly
pagan-rooted festival come from the very Jewish
readings for the day:

1. All Saints is a celebration of our communal
identity as a "holy people" rather than a parade of
individual saints. The readings are replete with
multitudes and crowds. In the first reading (Rv
7:2-4,9-14) there are two multitudes (though some
commentators consider them one): the first is a
group of 144,000, which represents the gathering in
force of the twelve tribes of Israel; second is a group
of indeterminate size (a "multitude, which no one
could count") and of gentile character ("from every
nation, race, people, and tongue"). The responsorial
from Psalm 24 calls to mind the crowd of pilgrims

moving toward the temple. The Gospel (Mt 5:1-12) presents the crowd listening to Jesus delivering his message of freedom and hope.

2. All Saints is a harvest festival. The first reading calls to mind the "in-gathering" of the twelve tribes of Israel and deliberately plays off of Sukkot (tabernacles) imagery. Sukkot, which occurs about three weeks before All Saints, is a festival that calls to mind in-gathering both of the harvest and of the tribes in the messianic era. The sukkot (booths or tabernacles) built on this day serve as reminders of similar structures built along the fields at harvest time and of the temporary shelters in which the Israelites lived during their time in the wilderness. The pumpkin-cornstalk decor of the pagan Samhain and our Halloween is perfectly appropriate here.

3. This is a great day for processions. The first reading starts with an assembling of the twelve tribes from the four corners of the earth, which suggests an entrance procession. The responsorial Psalm is one used by Israel as it processed up to the temple. The processional flavor is that of Palm Sunday (in fact, the images are the same) with a little Dixieland thrown in ("When the saints...").

4. All Saints is a festival of liberation. The imagery reeks of Passover and Sukkot, both festivals of liberation. In the first reading, the 144,000 are marked with a sign that protects them from the four angels with "power to damage the land and the sea"—much as on the first Passover, Israel was protected from the angel of death by the sign of the blood of the lamb. Also in the first reading, the multitude appears with Sukkot symbols—wearing white, waving palm branches, and shouting

"Hosannah!" or "Liberate us!" And again in the first reading, the multitude is said to have "washed their robes and made them white in the blood of the Lamb," which calls to mind the Day of Preparation before Passover, when the men who sacrificed the lambs had to rush home to wash off the blood from their white garments before it dried lest they become unclean. The responsorial and the Gospel, which positions Jesus as the new Moses, both imply Passover and liberation themes.

5. Finally, though children cannot be out of place in any Jewish festival, nothing in these readings suggests this is a feast principally for children. Saints are us.

The Feast of St. Building

Occasion: *The Dedication of St. John Lateran*

א

T he feast of the Dedication of St. John Lateran
(November 9) is the one feast of the church year that
actually sounds more boring than 31st Sunday in
Ordinary Time.

No one in your church will likely know—or
care—what a Lateran Basilica is.

This is unfortunate because the feast is about the
proper relationship between God, people, and
buildings.

However, the feast does raise questions.

The first is why do we single out the Lateran
Basilica instead of St. Peter's Basilica or, perhaps,
our home churches?

Obviously, the latter choice would put an
emphasis on the local community, which is
uncharacteristic of the Roman church. But why not
St. Peter's, which is the popular architectural symbol
of the universal church?

Apparently, that choice too is extreme. The Roman
church, in spite of its centralized tendencies, does
not have a central place of worship to which
everyone must travel on special feasts (or at least
once a lifetime). There is no equivalent to the temple
in Jerusalem. There are only local churches, which
have their own worship centers (also called
churches). The Lateran Basilica is one such local

church, though somewhat special in that it is the home church of the bishop of Rome, who happens also to be the pope.

Thus, the choice of the Lateran Basilica is an intellectually inspired attempt to have it both ways. The Lateran Basilica represents both the universal church (through its link to the pope) and the local church because that is what it is.

The second question is raised by the readings for the feast: why celebrate a building instead of people?

The three readings move progressively toward the idea that God resides in the heart rather than on a mountain. Even Solomon admits to God: "If the heavens and the highest heavens cannot contain you, how much less this temple which have built!" (1 Kgs 8:27) The scriptural movement coincides with current theological and liturgical emphasis on the assembly rather than the building.

The answer to Solomon's question has to do with our humanity. While God cannot be contained, humans cannot be uncontained. We live within containers: histories, bodies, cultures, laws, shelters. And when we approach an uncontained life, we feel lost, abandoned, adrift. It is a version of hell to feel oneself dropping (or even floating in) a limitless void. The longing for God then is longing for containment, a home, a shelter. Listen to the Psalm for the feast:

> Even the sparrow finds a home,
>   and the swallow a nest
>   in which she puts her young—
> Your altars, O LORD of hosts,
>   my king and my God."! (Ps 84:4)

In many ways, we are our containers. We are the history. We are the body. We are the home. So although St. Paul makes it clear that the new temple is the "body of Christ" (the assembly), when we are in harmony and not feeling adrift, there is no more difference between the church (building) and church (assembly) than there is between heart and hearth.

Solomon would have understood.

Part IV:
Prayer and Ritual

The Original Jesus Prayer

Occasion: *31st Sunday of the Year (B)*

א

Someone once asked Rabbi Hillel, a contemporary of Jesus, if he could recite the whole of Jewish law while standing on one leg.

Taking up the challenge, the great Rabbi lifted one leg and said, "Do not do unto others what you would not have them do unto you."

Rabbi Hillel didn't make up his answer any more than Jesus did when faced with a similar challenge. (Mk 12:28-34)

Instead, he quoted the Shema, a passage in Deuteronomy 6 that begins: "Hear, O Israel. The LORD is our God, the LORD alone!"

This phrase, which contains the fundamental theological insight of Judaism, is an equation: YHWH (the LORD) is Elohim (God).

This may not sound like much, but there was a time when tribal gods (like YHWH) were worshipped separately from the rulers of the universe (the Elohim). One ruled tribal history; the other ruled nature. But Israel came to believe that the Lord who delivered them from slavery was the same God who made the birds of the air and the beasts of the field.

If you think we've absorbed this insight, think about how many people you know who believe God is in the magnificence of a sunset but not in the messiness of politics. Or, conversely, about the

Christian social activists who think that protecting wildlife habitat has nothing to do with biblical justice.

The Shema is the rough equivalent in importance and use to the Christian Sign of the Cross. Observant Jews recite the Shema daily. They wear it written on their foreheads and forearms in strange contraptions called teffelim and they post it on their doors in a mezuzah.

Sadly, few Christians know anything about the Shema and even make the assumption, with some helpful misreading of St. Paul, that Jesus ditched the entire code of Jewish law in favor of two newly simplified commandments to love God and neighbor.

Yet Mark's Jesus, as did Rabbi Hillel, intended not to override Jewish law but to distill its essence.

Jesus began with the Shema and added a second commandment: "You shall love your neighbor as yourself."

The second commandment, from Leviticus 19:18, was literally a command to love one's fellow Jew, but, by the time of Jesus, it was extended to include at least resident aliens. Jesus, in the Good Samaritan story, pushed the definition of neighbor even further. However, in linking the two great commandments, he was being a good Jew. Like Rabbi Hillel. Like the prophets. The scribe approved of what Jesus said (Mk 12:33) precisely because he seemed to understand the prophetic tradition that practicing justice is more important than any burnt offering or sacrifice. (See 1 Sm 15:22, Hos 6:6, and Mic 6:6-8.)

This raised a question for me: If the second great commandment is not embedded in one's celebration of the Eucharist, can it even be the Eucharist?

War and Peace:
Two Liturgies

Occasion: *General*
ℵ

T he most powerful liturgy I ever experienced was in front of the University of Notre Dame Memorial Library in 1969.

It was a Mass protesting the Vietnam War. The focal point was a symbolic action during the Preparation of Gifts. Seven students, six men assisted by one woman, tore up their draft cards and placed them in a ciborium.

You couldn't get away with this today — the liturgical police wouldn't allow it — but it was good political theatre twenty years ago. Two thousand people watching, maybe a federal agent or two. We were in this together, collaborators, gathered around the Eucharist, sharing the cup before we marched off to jail.

The scene impressed me at a time when I did not attend regular Sunday Eucharist. I frankly don't remember what I felt at the time, pride maybe mixed with a bit of adrenalin, but the image has stuck with me and has become the measure of what the Eucharist can be. Risky. Political. Tough.

At about the same time, a friend of mine was in Vietnam about to experience his most memorable Eucharist.

Dan, a chaplain's assistant, and Father Gus were patrolling a paved road, looking for units that needed a chaplain. Off to the right, along a dirt road, they saw a group of APCs and tanks. They pulled off the road near the intersection. Dan stayed by the Jeep while the priest went up the mound, avoiding the dirt road because it might have been mined. After he reached the mound, the priest signaled Dan to come ahead. Thinking the priest was signalling that the road was clear, Dan headed up the dirt road. "I heard Father Gus yelling and screaming at me," said Dan. "I was confused. I thought he was signaling that the road was clean, but it was mined. I almost bought it." He retraced his steps and went up the long way.

The Eucharist has a way of being more poignant when your life hangs by a thread.

"It was beautiful, so peaceful, with the sun shining after a rain," remembers Dan. "Everybody was gathered around. There were some Protestant guys there, some Jewish guys, who hadn't seen a chaplain for weeks—and Father Gus slowed the Mass down so he could explain things."

Dan's Mass, like mine, grew in retrospect. "It really hit me when I got back home and went to Mass. Everything was beautiful, but people were just really out of touch. Our Mass was on an ammo crate, but it was real. We knew we might be dead the next day."

Dan's memory, and mine, reminded me that the custom of passing around a common cup originated with soldiers who had pledged to shed their blood for each other.

It is no accident that the Prince of Peace borrowed a line from commanders about to send their men into battle. "No one has greater love than this, to lay down one's life for one's friends." (Jn 15:13)

Playing with Fire

I have many memories of outdoor Masses. Several were celebrated on one or another quad at the University of Notre Dame during the Vietnam War years. Another took place in a grotto, accompanied by cassocked altar boys and fourth-degree Knights of Columbus. There must have been another one or two with the Boy Scouts. And maybe one in a stadium somewhere.

But one, attended by no more than fifteen people, was special precisely because it was outdoors and close to the natural world.

I had spent one October morning trying to build a *sukkah* with seven eleven-year-olds. Sukkah, the Hebrew word for shelter, is often translated in the Bible as "tabernacle" or "booth." Observant Jewish families build sukkot (plural) in their backyards during the fall feast of Sukkot to remind themselves of the years the Israelites lived in temporary shelters in the Sinai desert and of the harvest custom of sleeping in temporary shelters near the fields.

My sukkot are clumsy structures of poles lashed together, but they do resemble the rude booths you can still see in the fields in Israel and even in the Arab markets (*shouk*, the Arabic word for market, also means "booth").

The process of getting one of these things to stand always teaches me something. One day, when the lesson was on hardship, I erected a sukkah in the cold rain. I started with twenty kids and finished with four, who, once freed to race for the promised land of a heated cafeteria, toasted their newly discovered esprit de corps with richly deserved cups of hot chocolate. Those who bailed out, I noticed to my satisfaction, had no such sense of community. Their hot chocolate probably didn't taste as good either.

On this October afternoon, I had the usual hard time keeping at least one body on each of the corners. Every time someone tired and bailed out, the whole structure collapsed. We got it up, after many Middle Eastern curses on my part, and I understood a bit more about the way God works. The way I had it figured, God did not let the Israelites leave the Sinai until they could put up a sukkah in less than two hours—and it took them forty years to pass this test of cooperation.

This particular sukkah was meant to be part of the environment for a Mass in the meadow. It is the custom for Jewish families to eat under the sukkah; it seemed logical for us to celebrate Mass underneath its pine-bough roof. We couldn't fit everyone underneath, but we got the symbol going in the right direction. "We not only have the bread and wine in the tabernacle, we have the priest and the altar boys, too," said the priest. The tabernacle, which appears in church as a cupboard, originally was shelter from the sun and became in the wilderness a movable house for God.

As luck would have it, we had erected our sukkah in front of a fire ring. It is saying something about how far we are away from the roots of our worship that I hesitated to light a fire for fear that it would be sacrilegious. Fortunately, Leviticus got the better of me and I lit one anyway.

It was an odd thing to watch the bonfire roaring in the wind before a tabernacle, approximately where the altar of holocaust would have been in the time of Aaron. I realized then that, as a Catholic, I keep a biblical tradition lost even to Jews of my time.

I don't know what the others were thinking. I know the adults wanted to repeat the experience, and I know what I felt when, as a boy, I served at my first Easter vigil: Any religion that plays with fire ain't all bad.

Praying: The Art of Begging

Occasion: *17th Sunday of the Year (C)*
א

Lord, teach us how to pray.

You wouldn't think this would be necessary. Prayer, literally, is begging—something human beings learn how to do before they can walk.

But somewhere, God knows where, I picked up the idea that if you're *really* Christian, you don't beg. Especially if there's something you really, really want.

I know I'm not alone because the liturgical people I know break out into a cold sweat at the mere hint that someone might actually pray for what they wanted.

"Dear God, please kill all those opposed to ordaining women."

Prayers are not supposed to be divisive—a logical enough requirement in a communal liturgy—but the result is all too often passionless formulae written for ten thousand communities by someone with the requisite degrees.

"For our bishops that they may be filled with the Spirit of the Risen lord, let us pray to the Lord."

Snore.

The readings for this Sunday contain clues on how to pray. Not only are we instructed to ask but to ask again and again.

In Genesis 18:20-32, Abraham gets what he asks for on the first try. Emboldened with his success, he asks again—this time for a little more. "What if there are five less than fifty innocent people? Will you destroy the whole city because of those five?" (Gn 18:28)

No, says the Lord, and Abraham asks for a little more. Again and again. Just like a child who, given permission to stay up until 9 P.M., will then ask to stay up until 9:30 P.M.

Jesus acknowledges this image in his own instructions. How do we pray? Like a child, he says, asking, asking, tugging at the sleeve of Abba until he relents. We are not to worry about whether our requests are good for us. Everyone asks for good things. "What father among you would hand his son a snake when he asks for a fish? Or hand him a scorpion when he asks for an egg?" (Lk 11:11-12)

My favorite Prayers of the Faithful came out of the mouths of my sixth-grade religious-education students. Knowing that eleven-year-olds are adult enough to pray with their heads instead of their hearts, I resorted to subterfuge when our turn to do the Sunday children's liturgy came. I passed out paper and pencils and asked the students to write down one thing they wanted to be free from.

"Can we do three?"

Of course, I said, and emerged with a long list of eleven-year-old ills. They wanted to be free from homework, doing the dishes, feeding the goats, going to bed early, getting up early, parents, little brothers and sisters—and religious education.

Then I told them that this little litany would become their very own Prayers of the Faithful.

"Can we rewrite them?"

Like an old meanie, I said no and gave the wiseacre who wanted to be free from religious education the appropriate prayer to read.

On Sunday, he refused at first to cooperate, but under peer pressure finally he relented. His "free us from religious education" was barely audible, but his classmates heard it and the lesson struck home.

Any prayer of the heart—even what appears to be unacceptable—is acceptable at the altar of God.

Longing for Lizards

Occasion: *General*

א

Every time I pass through the Kansas City area, I stay in the room of a boy who is now twelve years old.

He is a boy like other boys, I suppose, and his room is a room like other boys'. Last time through, the room was full of dislocated underwear, plastic dinosaurs, and sports equipment. This time through, I entered something like a cave, bunkbeds walled off with sheets and surrounded with black and fluorescent pink posters of AC/DC, Kiss, and Motley Crue. And one squawking parrot.

His father is amused by the decor. "Why would a boy who is the gentlest, most sensitive boy you'd ever want to meet choose to sleep in an environment that can only be described as demented?"

Answering his own question, he suggests that the room is a safety valve for the boy's dark side, functioning something like dreams for those of us too civilized to put our reptilian thoughts out where visitors can see them.

"Of course, there is always the possibility that he really is demented," he grins, rather enjoying the thought. Twelve-year-olds are the dark side of parenthood.

If the father is right, then rock music is functioning as a safety valve for a generation of children.

But there wasn't always rock music, and, in fact, the music that accompanied a child's passage into adulthood was not always dark, and bizarre, and satanic. It used to be sweet and sentimental. Mostly about mushy stuff. Loving people forever or, at its darkest, not being allowed to love people forever. Even the Beatles made it big with "She loves you, yeah, yeah, yeah."

What happened? Sometime in the 1960s, there was a sea change that corresponded with, among other things, Vatican II.

Remember how it was before? Religion was dark, mysterious, and if not satanic, rather nasty. God seemed to exist principally to punish the poor fools who had the temerity to touch themselves in the wrong places—which, human nature being what it was, was bound to happen. Visions danced in our heads of 6th commandment violators being hung on meathooks with eternal flames licking their bodies. Confession, which saved us from this eventuality, occurred in a dark place before a human inquisitor and was, if anything, more immediately terrifying.

The last thing we needed in those days were lizards in our lyrics; we had them in our liturgy.

Along came Vatican II and God turned into love: A nice resurrected guy, sweet Jesus, inviting us all to supper. Altars became tables. Crucifixes became crosses. Corpus became a legal term. Confession became reconciliation. And everybody went to heaven.

Now children (that is, nine-, ten-, eleven-, and twelve-year-olds) listen to lyrics that curl their parents' hair.

My wife's twelve-year-old daughter says neither she nor her friends actually listen to the lyrics.

Right, and my friend's son does not actually look at the posters he puts up in his room.

As the father suggests, the boy needs those posters. And maybe he needs them because the (official) religion he's getting no longer has a dark side.

Enwrapped by God

Y ears ago, under the influence of Carlos Castaneda's *Teachings of Don Juan*, I discovered a special spot in my apartment that helped me to pray—assuming I "climbed into" it just so.

Unfortunately, when I moved out of Chicago, the spot stayed put, and my prayer life became irregular at best.

However, I continued to read scripture, which led me to Hebrew scripture, which led me to experiments with various Jewish pieties, one of them being the *tallit* or prayer shawl.

The tallit is a four-cornered garment worn by observant Jews for private prayer, synagogue services, and by some traditional Jews during all waking hours. It is primarily a male garment; females are neither commanded nor prohibited from wearing one.

We know that Jesus wore the tallit from the passage about the woman with a hemorrhage who touched the "tassel" of his garment. (Mt 9:20) He later attacks the scribes and Pharisees for making these same "tassels" too long. (Mt 23:5) These fringes or tassels (Hebrew: *tzitzit*) at the four corners are what transform the garment from a piece of cloth to a tallit.

In the Mediterranean culture, the tassels may have evolved from border ornamentations that signified a person's role and social status, which explains both the effort to make tassels ornate and the woman's extraordinary act of touching Jesus' tassel. By touching the tassel, she touched his very being.

The meaning of the four tassels, like many Jewish commandments, can only be understood dimly in the doing. Numbers 15:37-41 says only that looking at the tassels will remind the faithful of the commandments. For one prayer, the wearer wraps all four tassels around one finger. This represents the coming together of the four corners of the world and leads to a prayer for peace and unity.

The garment itself has its roots in the desert. A Psalm verse, recited before putting on the tallit, says:

> Bless the Lord, O my soul!
> O LORD, my God, you are great indeed!
> You are clothed with majesty and glory,
>   robed in light as with a cloak.
> You have spread out the heavens like a tent
>   cloth;...
> (Ps 104:1-2)

When teaching some sixth-graders about Abraham, I put on my tallit and tied a macrame belt around the crown of my head, thereby learning by accident that the Jewish tallit and the Palestinian keffiyah at root are the same garment. A great metaphor for peace.

Christians needn't feel left out. Some Jews wear a narrow, scarf-like tallit that looks very much like a stole. Perhaps our priestly stole is memory of this ancient prayer shawl.

But the tallit is a lay garment that is at its best when large enough to make the wearer feel enwrapped. Mine, cut from raw silk and decorated at the ends with meaningless fringes and at the corners with properly tied tassels, is 6' x 4'. When I put it on, I immediately feel at prayer, enwrapped by God, and living in the tradition of some long-forgotten ancestors.

As some of our vestment artists suggested, perhaps it is time to bring the tallit into the public prayer life of the Christian.

The Seamless Garment

Occasion: *Wedding*
א

Here's a principle: don't clutter your liturgies with symbols. Use one or two, and let them flow through the liturgy—and the season—like motifs in a play. One symbol, telling many tales.

Our parish liturgist is a master at this. For the Lazarus reading during Lent, he introduced a dance whose main prop was a long, white cloth that started as a funeral shroud, became a rope that tied the mourners together, and finally the altar cloth—for the entire Easter season.

This gave me an idea for how to use a similar symbol in my wedding.

I have worn a tallit during personal prayer for several years (see the previous chapter, Enwrapped by God) and had heard, somewhere, that there was a relationship between the tallit and the *huppah*, the canopy used at Jewish weddings. Both are related to the tent or, at least, to protection from the desert sun. In any case, the idea of turning a garment that sheltered me into a canopy that sheltered myself and my bride appealed to me.

The problem was how to incorporate this Jewish symbol with grace into a Catholic wedding in front of people who might be ignorant of either or both traditions.

First, I needed to establish that the cloth was, indeed, a tallit and personal symbol to me. Originally, I thought I might enter wearing the tallit. That seemed a bit much. Besides, our wedding was planned for Memorial Day weekend and my tallit would have been too hot. Instead, I decided to proclaim the first reading and don the tallit at that time. This seemed consistent with the tallit's use as a prayer and study garment and grew naturally out of my role as a lector and Bible study leader, especially of the Hebrew Bible.

Second, we needed to turn the tallit into the huppah. That took four broomsticks painted white, four members of my Bible study group, and a bit of choreography. But the transition seemed natural enough.

Third, I wanted the tallit-huppah to be a symbol for the larger non-Jewish community. So, after the intercessions, Carole and I accepted the huppah from the canopy-holders and placed it on the altar as a tablecloth.

In case any of this was lost on the assembly, at the liturgist's suggestion, I explained in the program the tallit and huppah traditions and suggested that our use of it showed how "Jewish tradition was around, over, and underneath" our lives as Catholic Christians.

Our use of the tallit was not the only element that made our wedding satisfying to us, but it told our story and captured the imagination of our friends and relatives.

I do not believe that the wedding canopy should become a standard part of the Christian service. For couples with no connection to Jewish tradition, a canopy would have no more meaning than crepe paper. But couples of faith can get similar satisfying results by remembering that symbols need to be few in number and like a seamless garment in which you can no longer tell the divisions between the personal, the communal, and the ancestral.

Louise, Jo, and Vera

Occasion: *Communion for Shut-Ins*
ℵ

I didn't know it then, but I've been a lay-prayer leader since 1978.

That was when I made my first visit as a eucharistic minister to a shut-in.

I cannot say I was prepared.

I didn't like old people, I had told the nun in charge, and I really was more interested in working with young adults. But either the ministerial pickings were thin or the nun knew something I didn't know. Anyway, I reluctantly agreed to go to the training session. There I spent a whole afternoon feeling foolish while we gave each other communion-on-the-tongue and watched a filmstrip designed to prove that the church began going downhill liturgically in 313 C.E. and didn't stop until 1965.

A big guy who talked about taking Communion to shut-ins touched me, though, and gave useful advice. Take along a church bulletin, he said; it helps shut-ins feel a part of things. And keep it simple; if an old man has only enough strength to get through the Lord's Prayer, so be it.

The nun in charge of our parish program had the wisdom to limit the number of shut-ins we could visit. Most had four.

"I'm only giving you three," she told me. "You've got Louise."

I took that as a challenge and liked Louise. She *was* a grouch, forever complaining about her housing and how her daughter neglected her, but I wore her out with my listening—at least enough to get in my communion service. Still I kept my distance from Louise, careful not to get sucked into running errands or acting as her advocate. One day Louise didn't answer her phone, swallowed up, we heard later, into one of the nursing homes we called the tombs. I wondered if I should have done more.

Jo was my second stop. Jo was not destitute—just imprisoned in a 99-year-old body. Her niece cared for her quietly, swept the floor while we talked, listened while I semi-shouted the Gospel reading while trying not to be distracted by the urine bag at my knee, then received Communion with Jo. One Sunday, Jo said she missed her sister. Tears filled her Cocker Spaniel eyes. I squeezed her hand, said I understood and wished I didn't. By the next Sunday, Jo was dead.

Vera was my nemesis. She was a crone, stooped from osteoporosis, crippled from a broken hip, with a body that collected like two sacks of oranges at the bottom of her nylons. She was a patrician lady—her late husband had been big in garbage—and she was a racist given to telling tales that hardly seemed appropriate in the setting. She cared nothing for the Communion or prayers, but relished the visits. Once she gave me $5.00 (stipends weren't covered in my training workshop) and eventually hobbled around every Sunday making me tea and toast.

Vera understood Communion, after all.

That was the worst part.

Final Blessing

Occasion: *Leavetaking*
א

Leaving Oregon, Illinois, wasn't easy. Oregon is pretty town on the Rock River, overlooked by a 40-foot statue of an Indian chief pretending to be a Roman, but mostly it is my home. I grew up there, left when I was thirteen, and moved back when I was thirty-one. For lack of anything better to do in a small town, I got more and more involved in the parish. I lectored, ran a Bible study group for adults, and somehow wound up with a sixth-grade religious education class.

The kids affected me most of all. I got the eleven-year-olds because nobody else wanted them. They were loud, ornery, funny, and stubborn—altogether like the Israelites I was supposed to introduce them to. I got to like them, and they got to like me. I was their teacher; they were my kids. We owned each other. My leaving was not something they could understand: it was not something I could explain.

We made do with ritual and ceremony. There were parties and hugs and exchanges of gifts. Even an impromptu blessing of my $100 car (it worked). And there was the final blessing.

This took place, naturally enough, during the dismissal rite of the Mass on the Sunday before I departed. An ordinary dismissal rite is both a commissioning (to take the Gospel into the world) and a blessing. That final Sunday, the rite had, for me, just a bit more oomph.

After the communion song, I received from the priest a crucifix as a symbol of my commissioning to go to California. I wanted to convey to the congregation that I was not just passing through. St. Mary's in Oregon, Illinois, was my home—a place to go out from, a place to take with me.

Then I asked for two blessings:

One from the priest, who gave me the blessing that Aaron bestowed on the people of Israel:

The Lord bless you and keep you!
The LORD let his face shine upon you, and be gracious to you! The LORD look upon you kindly and give you peace. (Nm 6:24-26)

And one from my family, friends, and students.

For the latter, I wanted gesture rather than words but wasn't sure if everyone would be comfortable with the biblical placing of their hands on my head. To find out, I asked one of the sixth graders how she would bless me.

"I would say, 'I bless you in the name of the Father, and of the Son, and of the Holy Spirit,' " she said.

"And if I told you you couldn't use any words, what would you do?"

She placed her hand on my forehead and made the sign of the cross with her thumb.

That settled that. I asked my friends to place a hand on my head and say privately whatever else, if anything, they felt moved to say. I don't remember what each person said or did, exactly, except that their gestures and their words were all in character.

It touched me most of all when my students, who were spread around the congregation, came forward to bless me. I had invited them to do so, but it was not something I expected from eleven-year-olds. I felt bathed in the good wishes of the people who meant the most to me.

Christians, I'm told, once considered the blessing to be a sacrament. On that final Sunday in Oregon, I found out why.

Part V:
Reconciliation

The Boys in the Corner

I had a number of powerful reconciliation experiences while teaching religion to sixth graders.

The most powerful of all was something less—and something more—than a warm fuzzy.

I always had food in my class and usually tried to incorporate the "treat" into the lesson. On this day, I handed everyone an apple and told them to hold on to it while we proceeded with a communion service.

Normally, I tolerated and even encouraged a lively exchange between the students and myself. Since this was a prayer service, I explained that their normal rowdiness would be inappropriate.

One boy, always a problem for me, decided to test this by continuing to talk as I began to read from the Gospel.

When I asked him to listen instead of talk, he rolled his apple onto the floor.

I fell back on my most effective disciplinary tack and invited the offender to take "time out" in the corner, sans apple.

I began again, and another boy began to talk.

I invited him to sit in the other corner, also without his apple.

By this time, it had dawned on me that I had separated two boys from the group while proceeding with a ritual whose very name spoke of communion between human beings.

I wondered what it would mean if I invited the boys back into the group for communion, what it would mean if I did not, what it would mean if I left them in the corner but brought them communion, what it would mean if I stopped the service altogether.

I finished the reading, invited the students to say the Lord's Prayer with me, and proceeded to give out communion—to everyone except the boys in the corner.

Then I told the students they could eat their apples while I told them a story about two brothers, a good one who stayed home to help in the family business and a bad one who ran off and got into a lot of trouble.

As I recall, a number of them did not think it fair that that the bad son got a party while the good son got only praise for a job well done.

But as I watched the boys in the corner, I pressed on with what the story meant right then.

"I feel bad that I could not give everyone communion," I told them. "Jesus would have given bread to everyone, and I think the story I told you means that right now God is with the boys in the corner more than us."

The boys in the corner gave me this funny look, and I dismissed the class.

Churchwrestlers

Occasion: *Reconciliation*
א

I have spent two seasons working in a process that helps alienated Christians return to the church.

It is clear already that this process leads to not only a formal reconciliation with an institution but often a resurfacing, if not a resolution, of old hurts and conflicts between people.

Once, for example, the group stayed for forty-five minutes in an intense discussion of one line from the Lord's Prayer: "Forgive us our trespasses as we forgive those who trespass against us." The line had raised the memory of serious childhood abuses that could not be forgiven by simply regurgitating a Gospel ethic.

Reconciliation is always a struggle, and for that reason I am particularly fond of the stories of Esau and Jacob. These twin sons of Isaac struggled as brothers do from the time of their birth. Jacob, the younger and craftier, always emerged the winner and ended up supplanting his brother as Isaac's heir.

Eventually, Jacob is driven—the Bible does not say why—to try to reconcile with his brother, who he has good reason to fear wants to kill him.

On the way, Jacob dreams the famous dream of wrestling through the night with an unidentified man. On one level, Jacob is wrestling with his brother. On another level, he is wrestling with his

God, perhaps the one driving him toward this reconciliation. The first interpretation is psychologically obvious; the second interpretation is given weight when Jacob receives his new name, Israel, "because you have contended with divine and human beings."

The metaphor of wrestling is powerful because it accurately portrays the sweaty intimacy of the reconciliation process. Arthur Waskow, in his book *Godwrestling* (Schocken Books, 1978), points out the ambivalence of wrestling, which feels like both "making love" and "making war."

But there is more depth to the story. Jacob is honored with a new name because he "prevailed"—something between winning and surviving—over his adversary. Indeed, he did prevail over his brother. Are we to understand that he also prevailed over God? His new name, Israel, means Godwrestler and honors him for making the attempt to win and for surviving.

But the struggle leaves him with a wound, a limp, so that he can never forget.

I presented the wrestling story at one session as a guided meditation by reading it over some instrumental music, pausing for long stretches at appropriate places. The long pauses allowed the images to sink in and take shape.

Next, I had the participants break into a small groups for a discussion of various elements of the story. I included such questions as, "Who have you struggled with throughout your life?" "Have you ever felt like your relationship with God or the church was a struggle?" "Have you survived?" "How have you been marked?"

The effect of these questions was to honor the story, which is to say the struggle, of anyone who is hurt or angry or confused by the church (or anyone else, for that matter). It also gave the group a metaphor for dealing with questions of conscience that come up in the lives of Catholics, especially. You wrestle with the church, honoring its teachings, and do the best you can.

At the final session, which was a communal reconciliation rite, we continued with the story of reconciliation between Esau and Jacob that immediately follows the wrestling story. In this story, the key motif is the gift that Jacob must give and Esau must accept before reconciliation can occur. In the examination of conscience, which also was a guided meditation over the same music, I tried to lead the participants through a process of identifying the Esau in their life and any roadblocks that prevented them from reconciling with this Esau. Once they had identified the roadblocks, I gave them a choice of leaving the roadblock in place and offering their need for the roadblock as their gift to the Lord—or of asking the Lord to remove the roadblock for them. This last approach, though unusual in church services, comes from an insight from 12-step programs, which has a separate step for deciding whether to keep or give up a defect of character (the sixth step) and for asking God to take it away (the seventh).

Confessions followed. I am told they were powerful.

12 Steps: Jacob's Ladder

Occasion: *Reconciliation*
א

What is going on?

Ray Kemp, at the Southwest Liturgical Conference, suggested that people interested in giving substance to RCIA should look into 12-step organizations.

A liturgist I know incorporated four of the 12 steps into a retreat for RCIA catechumens and confirmation candidates—disclosing at a later prayer service that she was the child of an alcoholic.

Come, Let Us Celebrate by Robert Eimer, OMI, and Sarah O'Malley (Resource Publications, Inc., 1986) includes, as one of the communal reconciliation rites, a model based on the 12 steps of Alcoholics Anonymous.

Joan Ohanneson, who writes most often of people hurting on the edge of the church, pointed out the phenomenon of churches renting their gathering and classroom spaces after-hours for "secular" organizations of healing—notably the burgeoning supply of 12-step organizations, Alcoholics Anonymous, Al Anon, Overeaters Anonymous, Emotions Anonymous, Sex and Love Addiction Anonymous, Cocaine Anonymous, Incest Survivor's Anonymous, and on and on.

I've been fond of pointing out that churchfolk are so ingrown that they can worry about people not using the sacrament of reconciliation, for one, without noticing how hungry people are for reconciliation. Perhaps I should curb my penchant for complaining. Some churchfolk *are* noticing that people are hungry for healing and reconciliation—so hungry, in fact, that they will invent their own rituals of reconciliation or flock to 12-step organizations that have a ready-made process of reconciliation.

Twelve-step organizations are not the only groups that are into reconciliation, but they are probably the safest and most effective, and the steps should strike a familiar chord for anyone involved in ministry.

See the 12 steps in the appendix. Look at the first three steps as a model for the catechumenate. I don't have room to print the full wording here, but in shorthand they are said to come down to: "I can't. God can. I think I'll let God." In some ways it is more complicated than that—and simpler. If you read the steps closely, you'll notice that what actually is required is an open mind (*maybe* there is a God who can) and a decision to take the steps required to turn one's life and will over to God. These are somewhat shorter steps than they first seem and put me in mind of what someone told me when I was struggling with doubt. "Faith is not the same as believing," she said. "Faith is acting as if you belief – even when you don't." In this sense, faith is not a feeling. It's a decision.

Next, look at the steps 4 through 9 as a model for reconciliation. Step 4 is an examination of conscience. Step 5 is confession (explicitly to oneself, to God, and to another human being). Step 6 is acquiring the willingness to give up the defects of character. Step 7 is a prayer asking God to remove the defects. Steps 8 and 9 are penance—making amends—which contains the idea of reparation and metanoia (metanoia is a change of heart; making amends is a change of behavior), and step 10 is continuing examination of conscience.

Finally, look at steps 11 and 12 as mystagogia, where step 11 repeats the apostolic experience of praying for guidance and power after the Ascension and step 12 is moving out into the world to be of service to others. Ministry, in other words.

What is amazing about the steps is not that they are logical but that they are taken by so many people who would die if they didn't. These alcoholics and addicts, victims of incest and abuse, remnants of lives lived badly have lived at the bottom long enough to listen: "...I have set before you life and death, the blessing and the curse. Choose life, then, that you and your descendants may live." (Dt 30:19)

Aching for Eden

Occasion: *27th Sunday of Ordinary Time (B)*
א

What can you say about Mark 10:2-16?

Certainly Jesus' teaching on divorce will appear harsh to the average contemporary community that is bound to include any number of people in various stages of marital distress.

Yet it is a difficult passage to skirt because it is one of the few that distinguishes the teaching of Jesus from that of the Pharisees who posed the question—or for that matter from the teaching of any other Jewish movement of the period. It is more rigid and less compassionate than anyone else's.

Jesus' position arises from Genesis, which he quotes: "God made them male and female. For this reason a man shall leave his father and mother [and be joined to his wife], and the two shall become one flesh.' So they are no longer two but one flesh." (Mk 10:6b-8) The Genesis passage is a creation story explaining the longing a man has for a female partner.

This story is part of a larger one, the Garden of Eden story, that explains the longing human beings have to return to an older, more primitive time before divisions existed. Israel, especially in its exiles, longed for this idyllic period of pre-history. So the passage from Mark is explainable as a messianic pretension: Jesus had arrived, ushering in the new age, and all niggling divisions were to evaporate. If the lion could lie down with the lamb, surely a husband and wife ought to be able to lie down with each other.

The subsequent passage about the children coming to Jesus, which may reflect the custom of children receiving a blessing from rabbis on Yom Kippur, accents the simplicity of the messianic vision. It is a new Eden, in which the messianic people are as innocent and childlike as Adam and Eve were originally.

We are not so different today.

Men and women still long for their "soul-mates". Hebrew imagery is more bodily: "...bone of my bones/ and flesh of my flesh;...." (Gn 2:23)

Human beings still long for God.

Human beings still long for a restored paradise.

Adults still long for the child inside.

And this longing, this ache for wholeness, cannot exist without the experience of separation. One must walk through separation in order to experience the binding of one to another—just as ancient people walked between the severed parts of animals in order to seal a covenant. (Genesis 15) Perhaps it is no accident that the word used for "making" (or cutting) a covenant and divorce come from the same root (*kara*). It is the people who have been separated—from each other, from family, from church—who best understand the power of reconciliation. Jesus understands this phenomenon, but he does not in this passage offer "sympathy," which was described by a parenting columnist recently as an ineffective strategy that leaves a child to wallow in her suffering. Instead, he offers a solution.

Act as if you were already whole.

Act as if you were one with your life partner.

Act as if you were in touch with the child inside.
Act as if the messiah had already come.

Theologian Mark Searle tells the story about a man, born into a secular Jewish family, who decided to become religious even though he didn't believe. Even so, he started keeping a kosher kitchen, kept the holy days, and said his prayers. Eventually, after many years, he began to believe.

The moral is that faith is not the same as believing; it is the decision to "act as if" you believe. It is walking and letting the heart follow, which is probably the opposite of the popular conception of faith. It is difficult—any weakling can walk a path they believe in passionately—but curiously practical. For if you wait around for your heart to change, you may have to wait forever. And if not now, when?

Appendix

The 12 Steps of Alcoholics Anonymous

1. We admitted we were powerless over alcohol—that our lives had become unmanageable.

2. Came to believe that a Power greater than ourselves could restore us to sanity.

3. Made a decision to turn our will and our lives over to the care of God *as we understood Him.*

4. Made a searching and fearless moral inventory of ourselves.

5. Admitted to God, to ourselves, and to another human being the exact nature of our wrongs.

6. Were entirely ready to have God remove all these defects of character.

7. Humbly asked Him to remove our shortcomings.

8. Made a list of all persons we had harmed and became willing to make amends to them all.

9. Made direct amends to such people whenever possible, except when to do so would injure them or others.

10. Continued to take personal inventory and when we were wrong promptly admitted it.

11. Sought through prayer and meditation to improve our conscious contact with God, praying only for knowledge of his will for us and the power to carry that out.

12. Having had a spiritual awakening, we tried to carry this message to alcoholics, and to practice these principles in all our affairs.

Glossary

Here are a few words used in various places without explanation.

Catechumen, catechumenate: from the Greek for "person instructed." A catechumen is a person under instruction for Baptism. The Roman Catholic church has revived the catechumenate, a long initiation process punctuated by various rites. See *RCIA*.

C.E.: an abbreviation for "Common Era," used by interfaith groups and non-Christians instead of "A.D."

Elohim: Hebrew usually translated as "God." Curiously, the word has a plural ending and originally meant "the great ones." Scholars attribute stories that use this term for God to the "Elohist" source.

Huppah: a canopy used in Jewish weddings

Kaffiyeh: an Arabic headcovering

Mezuzah: a small piece of parchment, incribed with the Shema from Deuteronomy 6:4-9 and 11:13-21, rolled into a case and attached to the doorpost of a Jewish home.

Minyan: a quorum of ten males needed to hold an official synagogue service. Christianity seems to have reduced the minyan to "two or three" men or women, perhaps because it was difficult early on to gather a full minyan.

Mystagogia: This Greek term, used by the early church, means mystery and refers specifically to the period between Easter Vigil and Pentecost, when the newly baptized struggle to understand both the paschal mystery and their own initiation.

Pharisees, pharisaic: The Pharisees were lay leaders who made up one wing of a pluralistic religious world in first-century Palestine. Apparently, there were many schools of Pharisees, but they shared the belief that Torah (the Law) needed to be interepreted as time went on so that everyone could fulfill the commandments. This made it possible for the Jewish religion to survive after the destruction of the temple in 70 C.E. The necessity of the interpretation of Torah has survived into modern rabbinical Judaism.

RCIA (Rite of Christian Initiation of Adults): RCIA is a restoration by the Roman Catholic church of a initiation process used in the early church. The modern process can take as long as two years and involves several rites culminating in Baptism on the Easter Vigil and a period of reflection (mystagogia) lasting until Pentecost.

Shema: The Shema (Hebrew: hear) begins "Hear, O Israel! The LORD is our God, the LORD alone!" (Dt 6:4) and continues with the commandment to love God above all and to post this commandment on one's door and bind it to one's wrist and forehead. As a result, observant Jews recite this prayer often, post it on their doors in the form of a mezuzah, and bind it to their heads and wrists in the form of teffilim. When asked to name the greatest commandment, Jesus recited the Shema.

Sukkah: a Hebrew word usually translated as "booth" or "tabernacle." A sukkah is any temporary shelter but refers specifically to the four-sided shelter erected by observant Jews during the festival of Sukkot as a reminder of the temporary shelters in which their ancestors lived in the Sinai and of the temporary shelters used by fieldworkers during the harvest.

Sukkot: plural of sukkah and the Hebrew name of the autumn harvest festival mandated in Leviticus 23:33-43.

Talmud: the oral commentaries on Torah that appeared after the destruction of the First Temple (587 B.C.E.) and were compiled in written form in the centuries after the destruction of the Second Temple (70 C.E.). Jesus lived in a time when the commentaries were passed on orally and some of his sayings (e.g., his comments on the sabbath) are similar to those later written in the Talmud.

Tallit: the four-cornered garment with tassels (tzitzit) on each corner worn by observant Jews as commanded in Numbers 15:37-41. Jesus wore a tallit,

tallit, as indicated by the story of the woman who touched the "fringe" or "tassel" of his garment. (Mt 9:20, 14:36; Mk 6:56; Lk 8:44) The seamless garment stripped from him at the crucifixion may have been a tallit. (Jn 19:23)

Teffilim: boxes containing various parts of scripture that are bound to the head and left wrist by observant male Jews.

Torah: corresponds to the Pentateuch or the Five Books of Moses: Genesis, Exodus, Leviticus, Numbers, and Deuteronomy. This is the core of the Jewish Scriptures and would have been so for Jesus and his earliest followers.

YHWH: The four-letter name of God, which observant Jews do not pronounce out of respect. Christians often spell the name, "Yahweh," and pronounce it accordingly, but the exact pronunciation has been lost. Nor is the meaning clear, though the word comes from the verb "to be" and is sometimes translated as "I Am Who Am" or "I Am That I Am" (Ex 3:14). Whatever that means. The Hebrew substitute is usually "Adonai," which means "mister" or "sir" in modern Hebrew and gets translated for the Bible as "Lord." Scripture scholars attribute stories that use this name to the same "Yahwist" source.

Y'Shua: the Hebrew version of the Greek name Jesus. It's a contraction of Yehoshua (Joshua), which means "YHWH saves" or "YHWH rescues" or "YHWH liberates.

Scripture Index